TEACHING TOUGH TOPICS

David Booth said that
"You get to be good by being with others who want to be good."
This book is dedicated to his memory.

TEACHING TOUGH TOPICS

How do I use children's literature to build a deeper understanding
of social justice, equity, and diversity?

Larry Swartz

Pembroke Publishers Limited

© 2020 Pembroke Publishers
538 Hood Road
Markham, Ontario, Canada L3R 3K9
www.pembrokepublishers.com

Library and Archives Canada Cataloguing in Publication

Title: Teaching tough topics : how do I use children's literature to build a deeper understanding of social justice, equity, and diversity? / Larry Swartz.

Names: Swartz, Larry, author.

Identifiers: Canadiana (print) 20190153377 | Canadiana (ebook) 20190153407 | ISBN 9781551383415 (softcover) | ISBN 9781551389424 (PDF)

Subjects: LCSH: Social justice—Study and teaching. | LCSH: Equality—Study and teaching. | LCSH:

Cultural pluralism—Study and teaching. | LCSH: Children's literature—Moral and ethical aspects. | LCSH: Children's literature—History and criticism.

Classification: LCC LC192.2 S93 2020 | DDC 370.71/1—dc23

Editor: Kate Revington
Cover Design: John Zehethofer
Typesetting: Jay Tee Graphics Ltd.

Printed and bound in Canada
9 8 7 6 5 4 3 2 1

Contents

Overview

Chapter	Featured Texts	Genres	Strategies
1 Race and Diverse Cultures	*The Other Side* *Skin*	picture book monologue script	thinking stems text interpretation
2 The Immigrant and Refugee Experience	*The Day War Came* *Escape from Syria*	poem; picture book graphic text	tableaux graphic page
3 Indigenous Identities	*Stolen Words* *Hiawatha and the Peacemaker*	picture book legend; picture book	Four-Rectangle responses think-aloud
4 The Holocaust	*The Promise* *All About Anne*	picture book nonfiction	visuals interpretation questioning
5 Physical and Mental Challenges	CBC News *Insignificant Events in the Life of a Cactus*	news report novel	opinion writing questioning
6 Poverty	*Those Shoes* *How to Steal a Dog*	picture book novel	storytelling in-role interviews
7 Death, Loss, and Remembrance	*Always with You* *After Life*	picture book nonfiction	oral narratives research
8 Gender Identity and Homophobia	stories on genderfluidity *Jake's Progress*	picture book dialogue script	sentence stems interpretation
9 Bullying	*Say Something* or *Dear Bully of Mine* *The Bully, the Bullied, the Bystander, the Brave*	picture book poetry	Character Journals choral dramatization
10 Ripples of Kindness	"The Little Hummingbird"	folktale	Readers theatre

Foreword

Building Empathy Through Children's Literature

This text resonates well with the theme of this book. It is an abridged version of a keynote address given by Deborah Ellis, author of more than 20 books for young people, on August 31, 2018, at the 36th IBBY International Conference in Athens. The complete speech, titled "Creating a Day Before," appears in the IBBY journal Bookbird.

Books by Deborah Ellis That Promote Empathy

Novels
The Breadwinner (trilogy)
The Cat at the Wall
The Heaven Shop
Moon at Nine (YA)
Sit (short stories)

Nonfiction
Children of War: Voices of Iraqi Refugees
I Am a Taxi
Kids of Kabul: Living Bravely Through a Never-Ending War
Looks Like Daylight: Voices of Indigenous Kids

On November 20, 1959, the Declaration of the Rights of the Child was adopted by the United Nations General Assembly. It states that every child on the planet has the right to live, to play, to be with their parents, and to be educated. Nearly 60 years later, millions of children have been killed in wars, millions more orphaned and injured, millions are hungry, millions are married off while they are still children, and play is a concept unknown to many.

As a writer for children, I look at the world and wonder, "What is the role of children's literature in all this?" I think I'm beginning to know. We create the world we have through our decisions. Our decisions are shaped by stories — the stories we tell ourselves and the stories we choose to believe that others tell us about ourselves, about our limitations and what we should fear.

The best of children's literature seeks to inspire young readers to create their own story of who they are and how they want their world to be.

Research has shown that children's attitudes can be shaped and enlightened through exposure to books. They can grow empathy towards animals and towards the suffering of other people. They can learn to see people who seem "different" as just the same with the same capacity for love, joy and pain as the child herself . . .

The best of children's literature can remind us who we are when we are at our best. It can remind us we need not be afraid of differences and that we have the power to create beauty out of pain . . .

Good children's literature can provide that alternative piece of information. It can provide a new way of looking at the world. It can be a welcoming sturdy branch that says to the child, "You have the power to choose bravely."

Good children's literature is not the sole key to a sustained livable future for all, but it is certainly one of the keys . . .

Deborah Ellis
Author and Activist

Acknowledgments

Thanks and gratitude to
teachers who have invited me into their classrooms to work with their students: Laura Conway, Marianna Di Iorio, Elaine Eisen, and Rachael Stein
colleagues and authors who have contributed thoughtful pieces that have provided sound rationale for teaching a tough topic
teacher candidates, educators, and students who have suggested book titles to augment my Great Book lists
Eleanor Gower, for listening and for giving advice
Cathy Marks Krpan, for kindnesses
Shelley Stagg Peterson, for neighborly chats and professional wisdom
Kate Revington, for sharp mind, sharp eye, and sharp pen
Jennifer Rowsell, dear friend who always gives me courage, and
Mary Macchiusi — couldn't have done it without you!

Permission Acknowledgments

CBC News, "The Class Photo That Made a Father Cry" (June 16, 2013); Deborah Ellis, for permission to include an excerpt from her keynote address at the 36th IBBY international conference, August 31, 2018; Firefly Books, for permission to include a graphic page from *Escape from Syria* by Samya Kullab (illus. Jackie Roche and Mike Freiheit); Nimbus Publishing, for permission to include the cover of *Always with You* by Eric Walters (illus. Carloe Liu); Square Fish Publishers, for permission to include an excerpt from *How to Steal a Dog* by Barbara O'Connor; Sterling Publishing Company, for permission to include an excerpt from *Insignificant Events in the Life of a Cactus* by Dusti Bowling; Margie Wolfe, for permission to include a visual image from *The Promise* by Pnina Bat Zva and Margie Wolfe, illustrated by Isabelle Cardinal.

Introduction

Tough Topics and How to Deal with Them

We need to remember how important it is to help our students construct knowledge about the world together as they participate in challenging, open-ended, imaginative, intellectual and artistic pursuits from various perspectives.
— From *Teaching Fairly in an Unfair World* by Kathleen Gould Lundy

If books could have more, give more, be more, show more, they would still need readers who bring to them sound and smell and light and all the rest that can't be in books. The book needs you.
— From *The Winter Room* by Gary Paulsen

The title of any professional resource is most often intended to spark an educator's interest to pick up a book and consider how it will support and stretch them. A worthy title of a teacher resource should synthesize the content, encapsulate the intent, and arouse enthusiasm to open the book, skim through the book, and ultimately, use the book. A title should quickly help teachers reflect on what they do in their classrooms, based on assumptions and curriculum documents, and massage teachers into thinking more about what they could or should be doing. Every dedicated teacher, novice or experienced, continually reflects on their practice and thinks about what they could do better. This reflection likely happens at the start of the new school year; however, an awareness of what is going on in the community, a global news event, a conversation with colleagues, or perhaps a purchase of children's literature can invite teachers to have their assumptions challenged. They can then contemplate what issues might be introduced into their program, especially when recognizing the need to teach "tough topics."

The title *Teaching Tough Topics* was ultimately chosen to inspire educators to pause and think about their programs, their learning goals, and their instructional strategies and consider what books they are using to bring meaning to achieve best practices for best learning. What *do* we teach? What *should* we teach? Who are the students we teach, and what do we need to teach them? This resource is designed to help teachers think about curriculum, what they choose to teach from day to day, class by class, and subject by subject. Is their curriculum framed by documents and subject binders? When I was taking graduate courses years ago, a respected professor, Richard Courtney, suggested, "Curriculum is what we do with our students at any given moment." Those words have stayed on my shoulders during years in the classroom and in my delivery of university courses. What is the curriculum we need to teach, choose to teach?

Before deciding on the title of this book, consideration was given to these alternatives: Teaching *Sensitive* Topics, Teaching *Challenging* Topics, Teaching *Risky* Topics. Aside from the alliterative ring to the three *T* words, *Teaching Tough Topics* was decided upon because the word *tough* seemed most appropriate.

Why Teachers Should Take On Tough Topics

Lundy's *Conquering the Crowded Curriculum* demonstrates how teachers can work collaboratively to build the four principles of inquiry, innovation, identity, and integration to form a framework for teaching and learning.

What makes a topic tough? Teachers might consider the Holocaust, death, poverty, and Indigenous identities tough to present, for example, because the issues make them feel uncomfortable or ill-prepared. A topic is tough if it might involve students revealing stories that teachers don't know how to deal with. It is tough if it might ignite strong emotions in students, arouse clashes in opinions among students, and uneasily represent digression from the "required" curriculum. Yes, most elementary teachers need to teach math and science and social studies and physical education and the arts and media. What, however, is the place for teaching the tough stuff which, according to Kathy Lundy in *Conquering the Crowded Curriculum*, is the important stuff?

We live in a challenging world, a world where we are called upon to respect differences and tolerate views different than our own. Being compassionate about others is a complex issue in society, too. Finding equity and a place of belonging is challenging in life and in the classroom. Furthermore, it seems that in this challenging world, more and more teachers are expected to deal with addressing mandated curriculum *and* finding the place for bringing the world into the classroom.

If our goal is to create caring citizens of the world, to build empathy, to deepen understanding of diversity, social justice, and equity, then it is important that we confront hesitations or perhaps insecurities we may have about teaching a tough topic. We need to challenge ourselves to gain information, gather resources, and introduce instructional strategies that help to conquer stereotypes. We need to find ways to have students reflect on their own identities and the identity of others ultimately with the goal of building understanding of tolerance, acceptance, and kindness within our classroom walls: values that can be carried on to living a life of empathy, acceptance, and caring.

When to Teach a Tough Topic

Sometimes life and school events have heightened my awareness of the need to teach tough topics.

Making Sense of Death

On June 24, 1985, I arrived at school on the final Monday of the school year to begin the day with the 35 Grade 4 students in the classroom. Before going into my classroom, I was called into the principal's office and was informed that one of my students, Deepa Harpalani, who had been sitting in a desk at the front of the classroom on the previous Friday, was, along with her mother and sister, on the Air India flight that crashed the day before and killed 329 people.

Shattering news. How do I tell the students the news of Deepa's death? How do I comfort them? How do I help them make sense of what happened and help them deal with grief? Always seeking a great book to support me in my teaching,

I got a copy of *Badger's Parting Gifts* by Susan Varley, and we gathered on the carpet as a community. There, I read aloud the picture book about Mole, Frog, Fox, and Rabbit who fondly remember their adviser and friend Badger, who died. The class then wrote letters and drew pictures and presented them to Deepa's father the next day. Varley's book helped me to teach a tough topic.

Bracing for a Bully

Once when I was teaching a family grouping class of Grades 3, 4, and 5 students, I was aware of troubling incidents within the school where a girl was continually harassing others. I felt the need to prepare students who might be involved in bullying situations and started with the book *Monster Mama* by Liz Rosenberg, illustrated by Stephen Gammell. This book provided a seed for gathering and presenting other literature pieces that would help students understand the complexities of bullying. (To date, I have more than five bookshelves in my office filled with resources on the topic of bullying.)

Over a three-week period, each book that I shared served as a case study for considering why people bully, how a victim might deal with a bully, and what the role of a bystander is. I provided reading, writing, talk and drama, and visual arts experiences centred on the bully issue, all with the goal of deepening student understanding of being compassionate and caring of others.

Challenging Children's Gender Stereotypes

Several years ago, as a Grade 3 teacher, I was concerned about the best way to help students understand social justice, diversity, and equity issues. One day, I overheard a student say, "Girls can't play soccer as good as boys can." The comment jarred me and inspired me to choose the topic of gender equity for an integrated unit. We examined magazine advertisements, considered which jobs were identified with specific genders (cooks, doctors, babysitters), and explored "boy" toys and "girl" toys, and "boy" books and "girl" books. The unit provided me with an opportunity to break stereotypical assumptions and have students consider gender equity. The novel that I read aloud to support my teaching was *Bill's New Frock* by the British author Anne Fine. (Opening line: "When Bill Simpson woke up Monday morning, he found he was a girl.") There were far fewer great books about gender equity then than now.

The Way to Help Students Make Sense of Tough Topics

Death, bullying, and gender equity were tough topics that I felt I had to introduce into my program. Curriculum binders did not tell me when and how to teach these topics. It was a choice on my part: I recognized a need to bring attention to certain issues in the classroom.

An airplane crash, a schoolyard bully, a sexist comment . . . How do we help our students make sense of a photograph of three-year-old Syrian boy Alan Kurdi, a refugee found drowned on a beach; of the falling of the Twin Towers; of hateful antisemitic graffiti spray-painted onto a garage door in the community; of teenagers who choose to end their lives due to hateful bullying on the Internet? These are all tough topics.

It is my contention that great books can play an instrumental role in helping us deliver the tough topic curriculum. Authentic instructional strategies will allow students to make connections and reveal their understanding. It is my contention, too, that great books can help us open doors and build bridges. As Deborah Ellis writes, "Good literature is not the sole key to a sustained livable future for all, but it is certainly one of the keys."

Books as Bridges

From *Reading to Make a Difference*

"When the reader stands in his own worldview, unable to see or conceive of any other perspective, a book can be a bridge. The right book, at the right time, can span the divide between where the reader stands in this moment and alternate views, new ideas, and options are considered."

— Lester L. Laminack and Katie Kelly (2019, xiii)

Books, especially books described as *multicultural*, can be the means to address tough topics that arise in the classroom, in the schoolyard, in the curriculum, and in students' lives. Some children's literature not only offers an alternative way of looking at the world but gives voice to people whose perspectives are rarely heard or, if heard, are not valued. An expansion in the publishing of multicultural children's literature has meant that now there are many more titles reflecting how some groups of people have felt oppressed or discriminated against. Children's literature increasingly presents worlds whereby students are exposed to how other people outside their experience live and struggle. Multicultural literature now focuses not only on matters of race and ethnicity but addresses such topics as sexual orientation, ableism, religion, and refugee experiences. It also celebrates individuals who act to improve the lives of people subject to factors that limit what they can be and do.

Whenever we choose multicultural children's literature titles for use in our classrooms, we must consider how well they address social justice goals, such as belonging, acceptance, and equity; foster a sense of inclusion; and confront intolerance. A list of questions to guide teacher choices appears below.

Choosing Books That Promote the Making of Connections

- Do the books we choose help students to see themselves reflected in the books we include in the classroom?
- Do we offer books where the characters look like our students? talk like them? behave like them?
- Are the friendships and families in the books similar in any way to students' own friendships and families?
- Can students identify with and connect to the struggles and accomplishments of book characters?
- Will readers meet characters who face similar or different challenges than the ones they have experienced (and can help them learn how to overcome those challenges)?
- Do the books help students gain an understanding of other cultures? abilities? gender identities? life circumstances? class structure?

In a classroom community of readers, students can meet characters both real and fictional who reflect or affirm their cultural identities, thus opening their minds to accept differences and opening their hearts to interpret differences with tolerance and kindness. Just as students are identifying with books they might call "great," they should be coming aware of new perspectives and understandings. The books allow them to see themselves as global citizens — to understand better their own beliefs, relationships, and values and consider how to act on them. If readers can understand that books about tough topics can inform and educate, and that an author had a reason for writing the book, they can better consider what makes a book great for them.

Authors Lester L. Laminack and Katie Kelly (2019, xxi) "believe in the power of reading, writing and conversation to stretch the known and expand the heart and mind toward a more inclusive and empathetic way of being." In their book, *Reading to Make a Difference: Using Literature to Help Students Speak Freely, Think Deeply, and Take Action*, they offer a framework "intended to deepen and broaden students' understandings, insights and empathy for the great human family and world we all share." The framework involves five phases:

1. *Selection*, when the issue is identified and the teacher chooses texts whereby students can gain insights into the issue;
2. *Connection*, which involves the teacher in creating a scaffold for introducing a character, situation, issue, or topic to the students;
3. *Reflection*, when students are prompted to reflect on their connections and notice similarities and differences from the characters, setting, problems, and situations in other texts;
4. *Action*, which calls for an event whereby students can react on their own and together to make a positive difference; and
5. *Next steps*, which focuses on fostering students as thoughtful citizens and life-long agents of change.

PERSPECTIVE

Why Use Multicultural Literature to Teach Tough Topics?

by Shelley Stagg Peterson

Multicultural literature is an important resource for teachers who believe that classroom learning experiences should make the world a better place by enriching students' lives and provoking their critical questioning of and action directed towards decreasing social inequalities. The enrichment comes from the vicarious experience of events and relationships in the lives of story characters from contexts that are unfamiliar to students. These contexts become increasingly familiar when reading multicultural stories, as students make connections between the realities, desires, intentions, and emotions of the characters and those of their own lives. As students read multicultural stories, they accompany characters who may draw upon unexpected resources and resolve problems in ways that would never have occurred to them.

Deepened Personal Connections

These vicarious experiences provide students with a window into the lives and perspectives of others and support the development of a deeper and more well-rounded understanding of themselves in relation to others. Through creating relationships with well-developed, non-stereotypical characters in multicultural stories, students can deepen their sense of empathy, a vital quality to provoke questioning of and action towards changing social inequalities.

Deepened Understanding of Social Inequalities

Furthermore, well-researched multicultural information books whose authors go to great lengths to ensure accuracy, who examine the complexity of issues, and who include multiple perspectives, provide useful background information about issues of social inequalities, marginalization, and oppression. This information contextualizes and further deepens students' understandings of the historical, environmental, technological, economic, and social underpinnings and outcomes of the unequal power relationships.

An Authentic Mirror of Students' Cultural Perspectives

Multicultural literature also provides a mirror, reflecting the experiences and perspectives of nonmainstream students whose ways of being and worldviews have historically been absent from children's literature. There has always been diversity in Canadian schools, with Métis, Inuit, and Indigenous children from 634 different First Nations speaking more than 50 languages and dialects. Children from non-Indigenous families have been bringing to Canada for many generations cultural perspectives, languages, and religions from all parts of Europe and from China in the early 20th century and then in more recent times, from all around the world. Despite this long history of diversity in Canada, teachers of past generations of Indigenous and immigrant children did not have access to the wealth of multicultural children's literature that is available to today's teachers.

The presence of characters who share students' cultural perspectives, values, and experiences in multicultural literature reflects a valuing of who students are and supports their creation of powerful identities. It is empowering for students to walk alongside a powerful character who shares their ethnicity, culture, language, socio-economic status, religion, sexual orientation, physical or intellectual ability, and geographic location. Students vicariously experience a sense of accomplishment and pride as they read about a story character's successful action taken against marginalization or oppression. Given the history of policies and practices leading to the marginalization and, in some cases, erasure, of Indigenous languages and cultures, and the significant role of Indigenous peoples in defining who we are as Canadians, it is especially important that children's literature written in Indigenous languages and reflecting Indigenous cultures be part of Canadian children's reading repertoires.

Unlike previous generations of schoolchildren, today's students can see their perspectives and cultures (and, in some cases, their mother tongues through dual language books) in the wealth of multicultural books published for children. It is important for teachers to bring this literature into their classrooms and engage students in conversations that open their eyes to the experiences and perspectives of others, support their development of powerful identities, and stimulate them to imagine and take action leading towards a better world for all.

A professor at the Ontario Institute for Studies in Education, Shelley Stagg Peterson is the co-author with Larry Swartz of *Good Books Matter* and *"This Is a Great Book!"*

PERSPECTIVE

Children's Literature as a Way to Empower Our Students

by Anne Burke

Teaching and creating classroom awareness of social justice is an ongoing challenge for teachers. Many classroom teachers strive to promote social and critical awareness, hoping to instill knowledge and empathy in students as they learn about current and historical wrongs. Teachers aspire to support children in taking agency for and redressing societal actions of the present and past. For example, many teachers are actively working to explore the treatment of Canadian Indigenous peoples; they explore a wide variety of resources to create these dialogues within their classrooms.

Children's literature is a great vehicle for allowing us to engage our students in discussions of social justice and diversity, studying sensitive topics, and learning about equity. Whether we approach the topics in a "gentler" way through the reading of a picture book, or encourage students to share ideas and understandings through their own stories, we can strive to create a working relationship of comfort, acceptance, and understanding, with culturally relevant teaching practices.

The Value of Culturally Responsive Teaching Practices

In an article in *Multicultural Perspectives*, researchers Ramirez and Jimenez-Silva (2015, 88) define *culturally responsive teaching* as "a teaching philosophy that acknowledges students' cultural heritage and builds bridges of meaningfulness between home and school experiences in order to make academic learning accessible to all students." Culturally responsive pedagogy provides students with an education that is both meaningful and culturally appropriate.

When we use children's literature imbued with social justice values to engage students in critical discussions, it helps children to challenge taken-for-granted assumptions, as well as to think about others' opinions and to consider why they may vary from their own. Pausing on a picture or passage during a read-aloud embraces the opportunity for reflection and encourages deeper conversations. It is a good way for educators to encourage and engage students to discuss their ideas and beliefs, and for students to listen intently to the ideas and opinions of others. When we embrace our role as agents for change, we seek to expose, critique, challenge, and transform the ideas and actions of those who are marginalized, working to provide equity and a voice and power to our students to make change.

Anne Burke is a professor at Memorial University, St. John's, Newfoundland and Labrador, and the author of *Invitations to Play*.

The Cultural Responsiveness Checklist

Teacher Self-Reflection: Think about cultural biases you may hold and make efforts to correct them.
☐ Read and discuss critical texts that celebrate difference and diversity.
☐ Read and discuss texts that challenge the status quo.
☐ Listen to students' responses and reflectively choose texts that consolidate social justice issues.
☐ Create space for critical inquiry.
☐ Create opportunities for students to become leaders.
☐ Create opportunities for students to become teachers about their culture.
☐ Create opportunities for students' voices to be heard in all aspects of school life.
☐ Create opportunities for students to become agents of change through school social justice initiatives.

Reference

Ramirez, Pablo C., and Margarita Jimenez-Silva. 2015. "The Intersectionality of Culturally Responsive Teaching and Performance Poetry." *Multicultural Perspectives* 17 (2):
87–92.

Organizing a Literature-Based Program: An Overview

The nature of a literature-based program may have a great impact on how students embrace the idea of reading. A literature-based program, like any other
area of the curriculum, requires long-term planning to determine practices that
will need to occur regularly in order to achieve its goals. Decisions need to be
made about what kinds of class groupings will best facilitate learning and how to
maximize the use of children's literature that teachers share with the students as
well as those books students choose to read independently.

Organizing a literature-based program invites teachers to consider the use of
varied genres as sources for learning and the choice of instructional strategies to
help them meet expectations. With an ever-expanding array of books to address
tough topics, teachers are encouraged to exercise care in choosing titles that will
help open up topics and deepen students' understanding of social justice, diversity, and equity issues.

The following components are essential to the development of students as critical and competent readers of literature.

Picture Books

Picture books are recommended for both the teacher reading aloud and students
reading independently.

Picture books provide an opportunity for a community reading experience.
Through interactive read-aloud experiences the teacher can offer opportunities for discussion about a topic, theme, or issue. The teacher can also use the
read-aloud opportunity to demonstrate comprehension strategies (e.g., activating prior experience, questioning, making predictions, making connections).
Picture books can be considered the foundation of literature and of the literary
experience. For young children, the picture book serves as a meaningful event
as it is read to them, read alongside others, and read independently. This vibrant
art form can also be experienced by older students, who can turn to it as a source
of choice for independent reading. Students can gather information through the
nonfiction selections or be captured by the story power and visuals of the narrative texts.

Thinking About . . . Picture Books

- If read aloud, a picture book can be shared with any age group. Students of all
  ages can enjoy listening to picture books. Even if characters are young and the
  situation seems simple, older readers can bring significant understanding to
  the themes and concepts by sharing their own experiences.
- Some multicultural picture books are considered more appropriate for older
  readers because the text, the narrative, and the images are strong. Two examples are *Rose Blanche* by Christophe Gallaz, which pertains to the Holocaust,
  and *Hiawatha and the Peacemaker* by Robbie Robertson, on an Indigenous
  theme.

- Interactive read-alouds invite students to participate in discussion by answering questions or sharing wonderings as they listen to the text. Most often these interactions cannot be planned for.
- Remember that both words and pictures can give information, tell a story, or depict emotions. Be sure to draw students' attention to visual images and invite them to share their responses.
- Consider nonfiction picture book selections. For each tough topic presented in this resource, recommendations are provided for nonfiction picture book selections (e.g., biographies, graphic reports, graphic texts).

Novels

There are three main ways to organize a novel program: (1) as a community experience, where all students have and read the same novel or the teacher reads one novel to the whole class; (2) as a small group experience, which may involve Literature Circles; and (3) as an independent reading experience.

The Community Experience. Teachers introduce students to material they might never read on their own. When experiencing the community read, students can discover new genres, authors, series of novels, worldviews, and cultures. Listening to a good novel read aloud one section at a time can connect students to a theme or themes they can discuss and explore in depth. Apart from the teacher read-aloud experience, each student is given a copy of a single title to read. Teachers can organize before, during, and after responses that include reading, writing, talk, art and drama, and inquiry.

Thinking About . . . One Novel with the Whole Class
- Planning and managing responses before, during, and after reading may be easier to facilitate.
- Monitoring and assessing student progress are controllable.
- As students share their responses with others, they can learn and grow from experiencing similar or different viewpoints.
- When the whole class novel is assigned, there is little or minimal student choice; however, the fact there is no explicit differentiation of ability or gender can help students recognize that they are part of a community.
- When students enjoy the community read, they may be motivated to read other novels on their own on a similar theme, by the same author, or in a series.

The Small Group Experience. Commonly, teachers form small reading groups according to criteria such as homogeneous abilities, heterogeneous abilities, social skills, gender, or interests. Or, selections can be random. Ideally, though, teachers organize groups in response to students' learning needs and common interests. Beyond that, the whole class experiences reading on a central theme (e.g., the Holocaust or bullying).

Thinking About . . . Literature Circles
- The small group experience can be organized by implementing Literature Circles. Most commonly, students reading the same book meet to discuss, react, and share responses to it.
- To promote full participation in literature groups, teachers can begin by assigning roles which will need to be explained and modelled. Students then switch role duties after each session (until formal roles are no longer required). Some roles include the Reteller, the Linguist (vocabulary and language), the Questioner, and the Literary Artist (illustrator).

Independent Reading. Students are given the opportunity to choose the material they read and thus their individual needs and interests are accommodated. Only one copy of a book per student is required; however, to explore an issue, students should select independent reads that focus on a central theme or issue. It is best to provide a consistent time each day for students to read independently.

Thinking About ... Independent Reading

- Respect is given to **choice**. When given choice, students may be better motivated and willing to read.
- Bear in mind that some students will need guidance on and support for their choices. Help ensure that all students are reading deeply.
- Since students are all reading different books, only one copy of a given book is needed. Students can acquire the book from the classroom, school, community, or personal library.
- Be sure to monitor and assess the range of reading behaviors and responses carefully.

Nonfiction

Nonfiction lends itself to independent reading, inquiry-based research, and teacher read-alouds of excerpts or chapters.

Schools have come to realize the significance of reading across the curriculum, especially nonfiction, and technology has opened to students much information and other types of nonfiction texts. We need to help our students notice text features in different genres, giving them much-needed access to those texts. Nonfiction selections are available for students to investigate topics of interest or concern; they serve to answer questions, raise new questions, and help students affirm or build new knowledge on a topic. Today, many young people choose to read nonfiction material independently along with (or in place of) fiction.

Thinking About ... Nonfiction Choices

You need to recognize that the nonfiction picture book can provide not only you but a community of learners and individual students with a rich reading experience. Consider the following criteria when choosing nonfiction picture books for the classroom library:

- Is information presented with both clarity and with innovation?
- What makes this book unique?
- Do the visuals and print text balance to present information about the topic?
- Does the book include a table of contents, a glossary, an essay, a timeline, or other text features that will support the investigation of information?
- How will the book support and extend understanding in one or more curriculum areas?
- Did the book touch your mind? touch your heart?

Poetry

Poetry is recommended for whole class and small group discussion, for independent reading, and for response activities whereby readers can dig deeper into themes and issues.

Those who teach poetry with passion and joy know that it can provide a rich learning experience for their students. As poet Sheree Fitch reminds us, "We journey to worlds and peer into spaces in our hearts and minds and souls through poetry . . . At its most serious, poetry rattles us to the core of our being" (2008, 4). In the past decades, great strides in the area of children's poetry have been made and those who value poetry can see it as an art experience that both entertains and informs through powerful wordsmithing.

Ways to Respond to Poems

- Writing about them: Use thinking stems to prompt written response:
  - I like . . .
  - I'm reminded of . . .
  - I'm puzzled by . . .
  - I wonder . . .
- Talking about them: Talk in pairs, in small groups, or with the whole class.
- Illustrating poems: Use a medium of your choice.
- Writing poems: Poems, in free verse or in a poetic form, can serve as inspiration or models for student-written poems.

Poems that uncover identity, relationships, and views can be an ideal resource for helping to arouse emotions and understanding of our personal and global worlds. Most poems are short but can arouse maximum thought about topics and issues. Poems can be shared with the whole class, or a poetry anthology can be offered to interested students to read independently. Using poetry can enhance learning, not only for reading and writing, but also for discussing, questioning, performing, illustrating, and movement.

Thinking About . . . Poems

- *Read poems aloud.* Poems can be transcribed on a chart or featured on a whiteboard. You can read the poem aloud. Keep in mind that poems are essential for choral dramatization experiences.
- *Introduce poems over time.* Consider offering a poem of the day or a poem of the week where students can come to discover favorites.
- *Build a class anthology.* Invite students to collect poems on a theme, on a topic, or in a poetic form. The poems can be transcribed and then illustrated.

The Role of Response in Yielding Fresh Insights

Through response activities, readers come to make sense of what they have read and make links from the world of books to their own life experiences. The variety of response modes that readers take to let their voices and opinions be revealed not only allows for individual differences in learning but also helps to develop critical thinking skills. Over time, readers in the classroom should be given varied opportunities to share connections, ideas, viewpoints, and questions about the literature they have encountered.

Keep in mind that we do not always need to ask for an external response. On occasion, the reading of a text on its own can be a complex experience. Students may call upon it later but have no need to respond at that time. Usually, though, students should do something with what they have read, perhaps through talk, writing, visual arts, drama, or media. In the classroom, we can promote and develop the students' responses by opening the text up for reflection and discussion and encouraging students to make their opinions known: opinions that are relevant to but not necessarily identical to those in the text.

Response activities that follow students' reading should extend and enrich their print experience — they should not take the place of reading. Students may be jolted into interaction and involvement with a selection after reading. Time spent with them in selecting activities that provide real reasons for a close text reading can lead to significant new insights about topics that may be considered tough; these insights deserve attention and deep understanding as students find their assumptions about the topic confirmed, challenged, or stretched.

Effective response activities result in students

- reading carefully
- extending their knowledge
- elaborating on first understandings
- discovering new patterns of thought
- interacting with others

Ten varied and creative ways of responding to a piece of children's literature are outlined below. These multimodal ways can be applied to books that introduce tough topic themes.

Ten Ways to Explore Tough Topics Through Multimodal Expression

With thanks to Jennifer Rowsell for this list of ideas.

Traditionally, response to literature involves oral and written modes. In the 21st century, it needs to encompass multimodal learning, too. Students can use technology, manipulate materials, integrate media and the arts, and create artifacts that serve to represent their thoughts about a text. When they engage in multimodal expression, they can work independently or in small groups to do any of the following:

- Create a Public Service Announcement that serves as an advertisement on radio, TV, or the Internet intended to change attitudes by raising awareness and educating the public about a specific issue.
- Make a short documentary about an issue in a book, perhaps homelessness, post-traumatic stress disorder, or gender identity.
- Develop a board game from start to finish — idea, design, usability testing, Dragon's Den–type marketing pitch.
- Transform a text (or excerpt) into comic strip or graphic text, perhaps using the program *Pixton* for their creations.
- Animate a favorite piece of text using a program such as *Toontastic*.
- Share an artifact or two that has a story (e.g., toy, a piece of clothing, a piece of art, a photograph). (Every object tells a story — students can find or create artifacts that help uncover significant elements of a story.)
- Write an interactive short story using the program *Storybird*.
- Create a collage from magazines about the life of a character. (What symbols, metaphors, or representations will best convey a character's life and the issue the character is confronting?)
- Create a digital story using *Storybird* to depict a day in the life of a book character.
- Choose an art form (e.g., song/music, dance/movement, photographs/art reproductions) that conveys the theme of the text.

How This Book Addresses Tough Topics

Teaching Tough Topics is designed to support and guide teachers through tough topics they choose to teach or believe that they *need* to teach. The nine tough topic chapters reflect an organizing framework for using children's literature to deepen understanding of social justice, equity, and diversity issues. Each of the chapters highlights a topic that may seem "tough to teach" but is likely something students will encounter. Teachers can find guidance in how to present a theme such as poverty in a way that will help students build compassion, respect, and care.

Each of these chapters contains the following:

Quotations from Children's Literature. These excerpts from novels, picture books, scripts, and poetry serve as thoughts to launch the theme. They are worth presenting to students before, during, or after exploring a topic.

An Essay on Why Teach the Topic. An authoritative voice, usually a guest contributor, provides a rationale for introducing the tough topic in the classroom. Some theoretical background and insights into how to approach teaching may also be provided.

An Introduction to Significant Words and Definitions. In "The Language and Vocabulary of . . .," students gain key vocabulary to discuss and understand the tough topic. Suggested activities let them explore words and clarify terms. They can draw upon their practice with language and word power when reading, writing, and talking about the topic.

Opening Up the Topic. Instructional strategies are outlined with the intention of activating students' prior knowledge and experiences; they are also chosen to arouse curiosity and raise questions to be answered by responding to literature.

Model Lessons. Two lessons in each chapter provide directions for using children's literature to address the focus topic. The model lessons, along with Great Books for a Tough Topic, serve as a guide for looking inside and outside a social justice, equity, and diversity topic through great books. Each lesson focuses on a certain genre and most often a particular title. It also focuses on at least one instructional strategy for exploring the text.

Resources for Students. Each chapter contains at least one line master. The master presents sources that can be shared to explore a theme, calls for students to identify assumptions or opinions, or serves as a graphic organizer designed to facilitate response to literature.

Great Books for a Tough Topic. Lists of recommended titles appear in each chapter to support the content of a given tough topic. Novels were chosen with students ages 10 to 14 most in mind. They address the diverse needs of students in a middle-years classroom (Grades 4 to 8), where there will be transitional, developing, and fluent readers. Titles identified as Young Adult are better suited for students ages 12 and up because book language or content is appropriate for fluent or older readers.

The last chapter, Chapter 10, takes readers past hard and controversial themes to present kindness — a combination of empathy and action — as something that teachers should recognize as curriculum and strive to teach their students.

Instructions for strategies are provided for specific chapters. A strategy, however, is not limited to one tough topic. It can be applied to address another tough topic, using a piece of children's literature that pertains to that theme.

Copies of most of the featured picture books, novels, poetry, scripts, and nonfiction resources help fill my personal bookshelves.

Chapter 1

Race and Diverse Cultures

We're best friends.
Even though we live in two different worlds.
Different, different but the SAME!
— From *Same, Same but Different* by Jenny Sue Kostecki-Shaw

"Ayden, you look upset," said Mom. "Did something
happen?"
*   "Some people called me a word I never heard*
before," said Ayden.
*   Mom was immediately concerned. "What did they*
call you?" she asked. "Come sit down."
*   Ayden whispered in Mom's ear.*
*   Mom gasped . . .*
*   "Mom, what does that word mean?"*
— From *My Skin: Brown* by @studentAsim, illus. Sari Richter

I do not know if these hands will be
Rosa's
or Ruby's
gently gloved
and fiercely folded
calmly in a lap,
on a desk
around a book,
ready
to change the world . . .
— From *Brown Girl Dreaming* by Jacqueline Woodson

I began teaching in the 1970s and was eager to build a collection of great books to bring into the classroom. My first teaching job was in a rural setting, a homogeneously cultured class of Grade 7 students. I was taking continuing education Language Arts courses, I regularly visited The Children's Bookstore in Toronto, and I talked with colleagues, including the school librarian, about books as I strove to gather good books that would engage my students and spur them on to choose and enjoy good books. In my early years of teaching, I wanted to introduce students to what I thought were great authors (Gary Paulsen, Robert Newton Peck, and Monica Hughes). Judy Blume's notoriety was on the rise. S. E. Hinton's *The Outsiders* was the must-read for young adolescents. Many students were keen to enter Tolkien's fantasy world or the horror books of V. C. Andrews.

How My Definition of Great Books Has Evolved

Thinking about it now, *Roll of Thunder, Hear My Cry* by Mildred D. Taylor, a book about racism in America during the Great Depression, was likely the single title on my classroom bookshelf with an African American character. Perhaps I bought it because it won the 1977 Newbery Medal. Was I aware of the need to invite my all-White classroom to read a story about a character very different than them?

A Seminal Read-Aloud to the Class

When I was in my fourteenth year of teaching, the novel *Maniac Magee* by Jerry Spinelli was released, and I chose to read it aloud to my Grade 5 students. This Newbery Medal–winning novel tells the story of Jeffrey Lionel Magee who is forced to live with his strictly Catholic aunt and uncle when his parents are killed in a car crash. The orphaned boy runs away and lives in the streets of Two Mills, Pennsylvania, where he eventually becomes a local hero. Maniac is challenged with bullying and racism in his encounters with characters who live in the African American east end and the White west end of the town. For me, this story, where students root for the homeless hero, come to learn about prejudice, and feel compassion for those who are illiterate, is a deserted island keeper of the best of great books. My students (not one Black person in the class) voted this book their favorite of the year.

I would say that this novel became a seminal choice in my career of book collecting. I set myself a challenge to find books that would inform and stretch students of otherness. And the publishing industry helped me, as it came to recognize the need to put books on shelves that represented the varied cultures of readers.

The process may have begun slowly, but in the past few years, in particular, books with Black, Hispanic, Latino, Asian, Jewish, and Muslim protagonists have been published. There are more and more titles that help students find themselves on the pages of literature and help open windows into the diverse lives of others.

Diverse Books and Authors Needed for Diverse Communities

For the past 20 years I have taught courses to teachers in the teacher education program and certainly in the past few years, the students in my class have become as diverse as any urban-centred community could find. As a middle-class, White male, I have become acutely aware of the need to find books that introduce diverse races and cultures. Choosing such books, I feel, shows respect for students who need and want to find themselves represented in books or to learn about others who are considered different from them because of their race and culture. Presenting picture books, novels, and nonfiction titles with characters of different skin colors, religions, and family customs informs beginning teachers, I hope, of the need to do so in the classroom, both in urban and rural settings.

Each year, I am approached by several teacher candidates who are genuinely interested in using books that deal with racism and anti-discrimination. They ask questions like these: "Do you have any books for Black History month?" "What do I say to a young girl in my class who wouldn't play with another girl because

A Young Girl's Book Campaign

In October 2018, Katy Scott of CNN reported a story about Marley Dias, a girl who, at the age of 11, had become tired of reading books about "white boys and their dogs." As a Grade 6 student, Dias launched a campaign called #1000BlackGirl-Books to identify books featuring people of color as protagonists. Over time she has collected more than 11 000 books and donated them to predominantly Black and underserved communities.

she said her skin was too brown?" "How do I help the student who hears the slur 'Go back to where you came from'?"

Serving students with literature that features characters who are different from themselves is a good place to start. Today there are many books written by diverse authors (Jason Reynolds, Walter Dean Myers, Cynthia Kadohata, Jacqueline Woodson, and Pablo Cartaya) who tackle typecasting as they present stories of racially diverse characters finding a place to belong. Many contemporary novels provide stories that help our students unpack the sensitive, messy topic of race and racism (*Wishtree* by Katherine Applegate, *Count Me In* by Varsha Bajaj, *The Hate U Give* by Angie Thomas). This is a far cry from the lonely title about racism sitting on my shelf in 1976.

How to Talk About Race and Racism

Choosing to talk about race is an option for many teachers and parents. Conversations about racism can be tricky and the context will vary depending on who is talking and what their personal experiences with race and racism are. Parent Toolkit, an online resource, provides expert advice for parents (and teachers) in *How to Talk to Kids About Race and Racism*. A few key points are noted below:

- *Set the example.* We need to feel comfortable discussing race and racism among ourselves.
- *Help children navigate their curiosity.* Encourage students to ask questions about otherness as they meet it in life and in literature.
- *Make it relatable.* An activity that calls upon children to make a tangled web involving balls of string can teach them how creating racism is easy but untangling it is hard for people who want society to be fair.
- *Be open about addressing mistakes.* Encourage honest communication about a put-down, rather than just calling someone "racist." "Tell me more" invites opportunities to share a point of view.
- *Be an advocate.* Don't just say people are equal, but act in ways that reflect that thinking.

Our classrooms need to be places where every student feels safe. Teachers can help students recognize that they are both similar to and different than the person who sits alongside them. Introducing the concept of "racism" may be scary, especially if the student could be the target of racism; however, doing so is essential. We must empower children to understand what it means to be racist, to confront others who are behaving as racists, and to work towards challenging stereotypes and talking honestly about race and culture. All this will be done with the hope of someday overcoming racism in society.

In the feature that follows, Michelle Grace-Williams discusses why even young children can and should understand what racism is so that deficit racial messages will affect them less.

Challenging Racism: Developing Children's Critical Racial Literacy

by Michelle Grace-Williams

> **Tricia:** *What do you want to eat, my little princess?*
> **Sasha:** *I'm not a princess, mummy. I'm not white!*

The preceding dialogue between Tricia, a Black mother and an early childhood educator, and Sasha, her four-year-old daughter who had recently begun attending Pre-K, reveals that children often begin to internalize deficit perspectives about their racial identity at an early age. Sasha's statement reveals that she is beginning to associate whiteness with societal standards of beauty. Since children are exposed to racial stereotypes at an early age, it must be interrupted in the classroom during these early years. Being color blind and silent about racism keeps the status quo intact to the detriment of racialized children and their families (Boutte 2015; Grace-Williams 2018; hooks 1994; Ladson-Billings 2009; Lyiscott 2017).

Children Can Handle Talk About Racism

My conversations with Tricia and my teacher candidates often reveal their struggle to identify ways of engaging children in conversations about racism and other forms of discrimination because they assume that children are too young to understand and handle these issues. However, several research studies reveal that children can engage in critical conversations about racism — something that is necessary for interrupting the reproduction of racism (Boutte and Muller 2018; Hagerman 2019). As Kaczmarczyk, Allee-Herndon, and Roberts (2019) argue, "Safe, effective conversations depend on teachers knowing that normalizing whiteness likely shuts down important explorations of past and present racial diversity, power, and oppression" (524).

Below are useful tips for beginning this journey:

Engaging in Anti-discriminatory Teaching: Tips

- Acknowledge and plan for ethnic-racial diversity in the classroom.
- Critically reflect on and address deficit teacher narratives, assumptions, and low expectations of racialized students.
- Engage students in critical racial literacy activities to raise their critical awareness.
- Select children's literature that represents diverse racialized groups positively.
- Consider including the silenced perspectives of racialized students and their families in planning lessons and choosing textbooks and resources.
- Promote children's voices and action against racism and other forms of discrimination.
- Collaborate with critical scholars, educators, parents, and community members to construct inclusive lessons.

Why Early Conversations About Racism Are Essential

"Not seeing one's self, or representation of one's culture, in literature can activate feelings of marginalization and cause students to question their place within society."

— Susan M. Landt (2006, 294)

Children are often observers and recipients of racism. Thus, delaying conversations about racism in the classroom is tantamount to delaying the support they need to understand this issue, cope with it, and address it. In this vein, though they do not fully understand the complexities involved, racialized children face challenges and internalization of deficit racial messages that will often impact their academic performance and psychological well-being. Thus, teachers must help to interrupt the cycle of oppression they face by engaging in anti-discriminatory teaching. When teachers embrace this liberating approach, racialized children like Sasha will begin to learn to see themselves positively.

References

Boutte, Gloria Swindler. 2016. *Educating African American Students: And How Are the Children?* London: Routledge.

Boutte, Gloria, and Meir Muller. 2018. "Engaging Children in Conversations About Oppression Using Children's Literature." *Talking Points* 30 (1): 2–9.

Grace-Williams, Michelle. 2018. "How to Inspire Black Youth in America Using Counterspace Pedagogy." *Black History Bulletin* 81 (2): 18–21.

Hagerman, Margaret A. (2019). "Conversations with Kids About Race." *Phi Delta Kappan* 100 (7): 17–21.

hooks, bell. 1994. *Teaching to Transgress: Education as the Practice of Freedom.* New York: Routledge.

Kaczmarczyk, Annemarie, Karyn Allee-Herndon, and Sherron Killingsworth Roberts. 2019. "Using Literacy Approaches to Begin the Conversation on Racial Illiteracy." *Reading Teacher* 72 (4): 523–28.

Ladson-Billings, Gloria. 2009. *The Dreamkeepers: Successful Teachers of African American Children.* San Francisco: Jossey-Bass.

Lyiscott, Jamila. 2017. "Racial Identity and Liberation Literacies in the Classroom." *English Journal* 106 (4): 47–53.

Michelle Grace-Williams is an instructor in anti-discriminatory education at the Ontario Institute for Studies in Education.

PERSPECTIVE

Multicultural Books and Critical Reading as Mirrors, Windows, and Doors

by Maria José Botelho

The metaphors of mirrors, windows, and doors have a long-standing relationship with multicultural children's literature. Children's books can serve as mirrors of readers' cultural identities and experiences. They also can function as windows into other cultural circumstances. The readers' imagination can transform the window into "a sliding glass door" as they step into worlds created by the words and/or images of the text (Bishop 1990). This transformation can deepen and expand the readers' understanding of cultural communities. Consequently, literature can affirm and diversify readers' lived experiences.

These metaphors demand that teachers reconsider *what to read*, that is, who is represented, under-represented, misrepresented, and invisible in the curriculum and on their classroom bookshelves. Multicultural children's books about or by under-represented communities of color, such as Aboriginal, African American, and Asian Canadian, offer counter-narratives to the ever-present White, middle-class, monolingual storylines. Several caveats can support teachers' use of multicultural children's literature.

Caveats About the Use of Multicultural Children's Literature

First, one book cannot represent a cultural experience because there is diversity within and among cultural groups. This caveat unsettles fictive unities within cultural groups. For example, all European Canadians are not represented in children's literature. The Portuguese Canadian experience is rarely rendered in children's books.

Second, race and ethnicity should be at the centre of any multicultural literature discussion. Whenever relevant, these power relations should be considered alongside class, gender, language, and sexuality.

Third, multicultural books are not immune to stereotypes and dominant worldviews. Children's books are cultural products, records of the worldviews and publishing practices of the time in which they were produced.

Last, although multicultural children's literature brings readers up close to the experiences of cultural groups, these circumstances are often represented as just personal and cultural. These multicultural texts should be analyzed alongside and beyond other texts. Narrations, monologues, dialogues, and plotlines should be examined within the power relations of race, class, gender, language, and sexuality.

The Necessity of Critical Engagement

These caveats demonstrate that teachers must attend to not just *what to read* but also *how to read*. The meaning in these texts is made through readers' critical engagement with them. Building on reader response practices that draw on readers' prior knowledge of cultural themes and text types creates spaces for critical engagement with multicultural books (Cai 2008). Recontextualizing the reader–text interaction within a broader context enlists the readers' lived and literary experiences as well as historical and socio-political factors as resources for text analysis.

Critical engagement with multicultural books demands that the metaphors of mirrors, windows, and doors be reframed within a broader context, too. Books as mirrors magnify how society is organized. As windows, they offer a panoramic view of how power is exercised among characters through their words and images. Children's literature as doors serves as entry points to examine how power relations can be reconstructed, informed by the readers' new understandings. These reclaimed metaphors of multicultural children's literature can guide the reading of culture and power relations and create a site for readers to become aware of how texts position them (hail them who to be and not be) and reposition themselves as researchers and makers of language, literature, and culture.

Critical engagement with multicultural literature becomes mirrors, windows, and doors into readers' lives and how cultures work and is constructed socio-politically and historically.

The multi-layered critical multicultural analytical practices (Botelho 2015; Botelho and Rudman 2009) offer tools to examine how books represent cultures and power relations:

From *"Multiplication Is for White People"*

"If the curriculum we use to teach our children does not connect in positive ways to the culture young people bring to school, it is doomed to failure."

— Lisa Delpit (2013, 23)

Critical Multicultural Analysis of Children's Literature by Maria José Botelho and Masha Kabakow Rudman (2009) provides critical analysis and philosophical insights for teaching literature, constructing curriculum, and taking up issues of diversity and social justice.

An online resource to support teachers' critical multicultural teaching of multicultural and international children's literature can be found at https://doors2world.umass.edu.

Maria José Botelho teaches at the University of Massachusetts, Amherst.

- How do the book's design elements (e.g., book cover, jacket, front matter, spreads, typography, medium) shape how the story is told or the information represented?
- How do the book's literary elements (e.g., point of view, social processes among the characters, story ending, genre(s)) shape how the story is told or the information represented?
- In what ways do socio-political and historical contexts offer insights for reading these texts critically and multiculturally?

The production and teaching of multicultural children's literature generate silences and render some cultural experiences invisible. All cultures deserve to be represented in children's literature because it is through these representations that cultural members negotiate their identities (Hall 1996). While multicultural children's literature can stretch readers' cultural imaginations, its integration in curriculum alone will not consider misrepresentations, under-representations, and invisibilities. It is through critical engagement with these texts that readers develop complex understandings of culture and socio-political and historical imaginations.

References

Bishop, Rudine Sims. 1990. "Mirrors, Windows, and Sliding Glass Doors." *Perspectives: Choosing and Using Books for the Classroom* 6 (3): ix–xi.

Botelho, Maria José. 2015. "Learning from/with Multicultural Children's Literature." In *The Sage Guide to Curriculum in Education*, edited by Ming Fang He, Brian D. Schultz, and William H. Schubert, 268–75. Thousand Oaks, CA: Sage.

Botelho, Maria José, and Masha Kabakow Rudman. 2009. *Critical Multicultural Analysis of Children's Literature: Mirrors, Windows, and Doors*. New York: Routledge.

Cai, Mingshui. 2008. "Transactional Theory and the Study of Multicultural Literature." *Language Arts* 85 (3): 212–20.

Hall, Stuart. 1996. "Who Needs 'Identity'?" In *Questions of Cultural Identity*, edited by Stuart Hall and Paul du Gay, 1–17. Thousand Oaks, CA: Sage.

The Language and Vocabulary of Race and Diverse Cultures

1. As a way for students to carefully consider their assumptions, prompt them to search for definitions of these three words: *race, racism,* and *racist.* Alternatively, provide them with the following explanations to confirm or challenge their assumptions about what these words mean.
   - A **race** is one of the major groups into which human beings can be defined according to their physical characteristics. The term *race* refers to groups of people who have differences and similarities in biological traits deemed by society to be socially significant; in other words, people treat other people differently because of them. The most widely used human racial types are based on visual traits (skin color, facial features, type of hair).
   - **Racism** is prejudice, discrimination, or antagonism directed against someone of a different race based on the belief that one's own race is superior.
   - A **racist** is a person who shows or feels discrimination or prejudice against other people of other races, or who believes that a particular race is superior to another.
2. Meanings of the words *race* and *ethnicity* are sometimes confused. Draw students' attention to the words and what they each mean.

- **Race** refers to a person's physical characteristics, such as bone structure and skin, hair, and eye color.
- **Ethnicity** refers to cultural factors, including nationality, regional culture, ancestry, and language.

3. Invite middle-year or older students to provide explanations for the following words without referring to a dictionary: *prejudice*, *bias*, *segregation*, *discrimination*, *bigot*, and *intolerance*. Challenge students to write a sentence for each of these words that helps to explain the word's meaning or provides an example.

Sample Sentence: When he kept deliberately using rude words to describe his neighbors, he showed himself to be a bigot.

Opening Up the Topic of Race and Diverse Cultures

Students open up the topic of race and diverse cultures in two ways. In Part A, they read and think about hypothetical scenarios that are intended to prompt discussion about how they would respond to various situations. A variety of scenarios focus on the challenges of dealing with incidents of racism past, present, and future. In Part B, they look at the topic from the perspective of books they read and are exposed to.

Part A: What Would You Do? Considering Racist Scenarios

To prepare students for exploring the scenarios activity, be sure to remind them of the definition of *racist*. Provide students with copies of the "Thinking About Racism: What If . . . " line master on page 32 and have them read the statements independently. Tell students to choose one of the situations and write a response to what they would do in that situation. Students can then meet in groups to compare answers and discuss how best to deal with one or more of these events.

Alternatively, the statements could be cut into strips. Individual strips can be distributed to each student. Some strips can be duplicated so that more than one student considers a given situation. Students can discuss the statements in either of the following ways:

- They can meet with others who have the same strip.
- They can meet in groups of five or six and discuss how to respond to each of these situations morally and ethically.

Extension

As a class, discuss how each of these situations deals with the topic of race and racism. What advice would students give to someone who is a participant in one of the situations?

Part B: What Do You Think? Considering Book Choices

The questionnaire "Thinking About My Fiction Choices" (see page 33) is intended to help students consider their reading preferences, book choices, and opinions on reading *about* diversity. Students can approach the line master in one of two ways. They can either complete it independently or work in pairs to interview one another.

Once they have addressed the questionnaire, students can work in groups of three or four to share and compare answers.

Model Lesson 1: Responding to a Picture Book Through Thinking Stems

This lesson works well with students of all levels.

Any of the picture book titles listed in Great Books for a Tough Topic (pages 36 and 38) are appropriate for this lesson. *Last Stop on Market Street* by Matt de la Peña, *The Proudest Blue: A Story of Hijab and Family* by Ibtihaj Muhammad, and *Viola Desmond Won't Be Budged!* by Jody Nyasha Warner are especially recommended.

Featured Text: The Other Side *by Jacqueline Woodson*

The Other Side by Jacqueline Woodson is the story of a fence that separates the Black side of town from the White side of town. When Clover sees a White girl from "the other side" sitting on the fence, she grows more curious about why the fence is there and how its division can be conquered.

Thinking stems, or prompts, allow students to reflect on their reading and then respond to a text first in writing and then through discussion. They offer a convenient strategy for honoring individual, personal response to a text where answers can be open-ended. Each prompt can connect to a comprehension strategy. When introducing thinking stems, you can use either of these two methods:

1. Assign students three different prompts to complete.
2. Offer students a list of various prompts and have them choose at least three they want to respond to.

Here is a list of thinking stems to consider:

I know	I feel	I am reminded of
I predict	I hope	I want to know more about
I like	I imagine	I am puzzled by
I don't like	I remember	I wonder

Once students have each completed their thinking stems, have them share and compare their responses with a partner — it does not matter if students have responded to different thinking stems. Next, students can form groups of three or four and reflect on and discuss the text, drawing on other thinking stems they have not yet written about. The whole class can then discuss the text, sharing, listening to, and responding to different views. Consider giving students the opportunity to write a response to a text after a discussion where different opinions have been offered.

After listening to the story being read aloud, Marianna Di Iorio's Grade 5 class responded to the picture book by recording thoughts on what they felt, what they were reminded of, and what they wondered about.

I FEEL . . .
    embarrassed that this actually happened.
    angry that nobody thought the fence was wrong.
    sorry for the two girls because they can't climb each other's fence.
    frustrated because everyone should be able to be with who they want to be with.
    confused because I don't know why a person would build a fence to keep a black girl and white girl from playing together.
    happy because two girls with different skin colors became friends and could now sit on the fence.
    mad — racism makes me mad.
    upset that there was a fence to separate black and white people.
I REMEMBER . . .
    the story of Harriet Tubman and the Underground Railroad.
    when Martin Luther King Jr. tried to stop racism.
    the book the teacher read to us about Ruby Bridges who stood up for black people and went to a white school.
    Viola Desmond at the movie theatre and she refused to move from her seat.

The Need for Diversity in Books
Classroom teacher Ernest Agbuya and his Grade 6 class conducted an inquiry about the diversity represented by the books the students read. Here are a few pertinent findings:

- What is the race of main characters? (74% Caucasian)
- What is the nationality of the authors? (69% American)
- What is the race of the authors? (85% Caucasian)
- Where are your books set? (56% in the United States or Europe)

Yet, in Agbuya's class, only 25 percent of the students were Caucasian. The rest hailed from East Indian, Asian, or Black cultures.

Thinking About Racism: What If . . .?

The incidents outlined below are intended to prompt discussion on how you would respond to various situations. They focus on the challenges of dealing with incidents of racism past, present, and future. You will have a chance to respond to one or more of these scenarios and discuss with others how to deal with the event morally and ethically.

What if . . . you witnessed someone spray-painting a piece of racist graffiti in your neighborhood?

What if . . . someone called you a bad name when you were walking down the hall of your school?

What if . . . you saw someone on a bus turn or walk away from someone of a different skin color?

What if . . . you or a friend who is a minority receive anonymous emails that make racist comments? The messages were ignored at first, but over a month, they get worse.

What if . . . you heard someone telling a racist joke?

What if . . . you saw someone in tears due to being called a racist name?

What if . . . you saw someone in your school write an offensive message on someone's locker?

What if . . . someone made fun of you because of the lunch you brought to school?

What if . . . someone made fun of a friend of yours because of the clothing your friend was wearing?

What if . . . you heard someone make fun of someone's accent?

What if . . . you learned that someone new to the school was being excluded from membership on a team because of their race?

What if . . . you were assigned to be in a group where everyone else's culture was the same, but different than yours?

What if . . . you saw someone in a neighborhood store being bullied because of their race?

What if . . . you were told that a friend of yours wasn't invited to a party because of their skin color?

What if . . . the assigned novel(s) in your class had no character of a culture or race with whom you could identify?

What if . . . you hear some students from your school saying rude things about a good friend? You know that your friend's mother has advised her to ignore such incidents.

What if . . . you overheard a group of young children make fun of someone while they were playing?

Pembroke Publishers © 2020 *Teaching Tough Topics* by Larry Swartz   ISBN 978-1-55138-341-5

Thinking About My Fiction Choices

Complete each of the following statements to help you think about your reading preferences. Challenge yourself to circle only one response to each stem. Once you have done so, meet with two or three classmates to share and compare answers.

1. I would rather read fiction
   a) that has characters who are like me.
   b) that has characters who are different from me.
   c) that has characters both like me and different from me.

2. I would rather read fiction
   a) that has characters of the same gender as me.
   b) that has characters of a different gender than me.
   c) that has characters that are equally the same and different than me.

3. I would rather read
   a) more fiction than nonfiction.
   b) more nonfiction than fiction.
   c) fiction and nonfiction equally.

4. I would rather read about tough topics through
   a) fiction titles (including picture books).
   b) nonfiction titles.
   c) the Internet.

5. I would prefer to read a book about a tough topic
   a) that a friend recommended.
   b) that a teacher or librarian recommended.
   c) that I chose on my own.

Please respond to the following:
I can learn a lot about people who are different from me by reading fiction.

          Agree   Disagree   Unsure

Books can help me change my views on social justice, diversity, and equity issues.

          Agree   Disagree   Unsure

A fictional character much like me is _____ in _____

Good books matter when _____

_____

I recommend this great book to learn about diverse cultures: _____

Here's why: _____

For the thinking stems activity, students could also respond to a poem, a media report, a news article, or a nonfiction selection.

I WONDER...

if this is fiction or nonfiction.

what would happen if someone tore the fence down.

what the black mother would say when she saw the two girls sitting on the fence.

if the parents of these two girls ever accepted that their children were friends.

why are people segregated just because of their skin color.

whether the girls can continue to be friends in the future.

who taught the mother to be racist.

what the two girls would say to each other when they talk for the first time — what questions would they ask?

what I would have done if I wanted to go to the other side.

Model Lesson 2: Unpacking a Monologue Script

Featured Text: Skin *by Dennis Foon*

This lesson works well with students in Grades 4 to 9.

A monologue is a short speech that a character gives to an audience. The character might use the monologue as a vehicle to express personal feelings and thoughts on a subject or event or tell a story or anecdote. Most commonly, a monologue is recited by one person. As written, the script on page 37 is the prologue to the play *Skin* by Dennis Foon and could be read by one person, a pair, small groups, or the whole class. *Skin* presents stories from characters of diverse races. This excerpt honors the ties that bind us.

Interpretation of a Minimal Script

Whole Class. Students sit in a circle and read the opening scene aloud as a whole class. Next, each student, in a clockwise direction, reads aloud one of the lines. Then, the activity is repeated, with students reading the lines in a counterclockwise direction. In this way, students have the chance to read two lines aloud.

Students can explore this minimal script by

- reading it aloud as quickly as possible
- pausing between the reading of each line
- reading the script from whisper to loud volume
- reading the script as a round
- adding gesture as the line is read
- presenting the script in gesture or mime only
- rearranging the order in which the lines are read

Small Groups. To further practise interpretation techniques, students work in groups of four or five. Each group experiments with ways of dividing the lines (some lines as solo, some in pairs, some by the whole group). Once lines are divided, students rehearse the script by exploring and practising emphasis, pitch, and pace. They should also consider what gestures and movements to add. How will they begin and end the reading of the piece?

Paired Groups. Groups share their rehearsed interpretations of the script. Each group is matched with another to present their work and be an audience for the other group. Students can note similarities and differences in the presentations.

Improvisation of What Came Before

Discussing the Script. The class discusses the monologue script in order to better understand the message that the playwright was hoping to convey. The following questions can be used to guide the discussion:

- What does this script invite you to think about?
- What connections can you make to this script?
- What message do you think the playwright was trying to convey in those lines for a play titled *Skin*?
- Why would Dennis Foon use short lines and repeat some of these lines?
- If you were watching the play *Skin* in the theatre, how might you expect the opening scene to look?
- What event might have prompted someone to speak these lines? In other words, what do you think happened that might have triggered this monologue?

Improvising a Backstory. In small groups, students prepare a short improvisation to explain why someone might say this monologue aloud to serve as a prologue to a play called *Skin*. In the context of the theme of *Skin*, the improvisation would likely focus on an incident that depicts racism, prejudice, rejection, teasing, or bullying.

To prepare for the improvisation, students can discuss these questions: Who might be saying these words? How is the person feeling? Who would have listened to the person? What happened to this person?

Remind students that the lines in the script need not appear in the improvisation. The improvised scene is meant to reveal what happens *before* the scripted monologue is given.

Invite groups to present their scenes to share perceptions about the character.

Extension Activities

- *Hot Seating:* A student assumes the role of a character connected with *Skin* and is interviewed by classmates who want to discover more about the character.
- *One Way to Write a Monologue:* Prompt students to become a character from their improvised scene. Tell them to imagine that this character keeps a diary or journal for recording thoughts and feelings. Students write a diary entry as if they were the character. Once they have done so, they can read the entry aloud. Because the piece was written in the first person, entries can serve as monologues for students to rehearse and present.
- *Continuing the Script:* Students work independently or with a partner to continue the script by adding 10 to 12 lines that would give more information about the character. Line lengths can vary.
- *Exploring the Script:* If the text is available, students work with other scenes that appear in the script *Skin*. Each scene depicts an aspect of racism or prejudice.

Ideas presented here appear in an August 12, 2019, article by Kim Snider for EdCan Network. The full article, "The 3 R's of Diversifying Your Classroom Booklist," can be found at http://www.edcan.ca/articles/diversifying-your-classroom-booklist.

Great Books for a Tough Topic

Emergence of a Great Book

The Snowy Day, awarded the 1963 Caldecott Medal, was named one of the 100 most important books of the 20th century by the New York Public Library. In his Caldecott speech, Ezra Jack Keats said, "I can honestly say that Peter [the book's hero, a little Black boy] came into being because we wanted him." Up until *The Snowy Day*, African American children did not see others like themselves in children's books. More than 50 years later, the book industry has exploded with books that shine a light on race, culture, and identity.

Great in the sense it is used here and throughout this resource denotes a book that will have a significant impact on students: an impact that will endure long after they have heard, read, or responded to the text. Young readers react differently to the books they are exposed to. To affirm that "this is a great book!" means that the child, the context, the occasion, and the culture all work together.

Picture Books

Barnes, Derrick (illus. Gordon C. James). *Crown: An Ode to the Fresh Cut*
De la Peña, Matt (illus. Christian Robinson). *Last Stop on Market Street*
Diggs, Taye (illus. Shane W. Evans). *Chocolate Me!*
Franklin, Ashley (illus. Ebony Glenn). *Not Quite Snow White*
Gonzales, Mark (illus. Mehrdokht Amini). *Yo Soy Muslim: A Father's Letter to His Daughter*

Skin by Dennis Foon: An Excerpt

I am five foot six inches tall.

I weigh 250 pounds.

I have two arms.

Two legs

Two feet

Two ears

Two eyes

One nose

One mouth

Ten fingers

Ten toes.

I can taste.

I can smell.

I can see.

I can hear.

I can touch.

My blood is red.

My blood is red.

My blood is red.

My blood is red.

I breathe.

I think.

I feel.

I feel.

I feel.

I feel.

Pembroke Publishers © 2020 *Teaching Tough Topics* by Larry Swartz   ISBN 978-1-55138-341-5

Giovanni, Nikki (illus. Bryan Collier). *Rosa*

Hall, Michael. *Red: A Crayon's Story*

hooks, bell (illus. Chris Raschka). *Skin Again*

Keats, Ezra Jack. *The Snowy Day*

Khan, Hena (illus. Aaliya Jaleel). *Under My Hijab*

Kostecki-Shaw, Jenny Sue. *Same, Same but Different*

Lester, Julius (illus. Karen Barbour). *Let's Talk About Race*

Martinez-Neal, Juana. *Alma and How She Got Her Name*

Mobin-Uddin, Asma (illus. Barbara Kiwak). *My Name Is Bilal*

Muhammad, Ibtihaj, with S. K. Ali (illus. Hatem Aly). *The Proudest Blue: A Story of Hijab and Family*

Parr, Todd. *It's Okay to Be Different*

Polacco, Patricia. *Mr. Lincoln's Way* (Also: *January's Sparrow*; *Pink and Say*)

Stehlik, Tania Duprey (illus. Vanja Nuleta Jovanovic). *Violet*

@studentAsim (illus. Sari Richter). *My Skin: Brown*

Tonatiuh, Duncan. *Separate Is Never Equal: Sylvia Mendez and Her Family's Fight for Desegregation*

Warner, Jody Nyasha (illus. Richard Rudnicki). *Viola Desmond Won't Be Budged!*

Weatherford, Carole Boston (illus. Kadir Nelson). *Moses: When Harriet Tubman Led Her People to Freedom*

Winter, Jeanette. *Malala: A Brave Girl from Pakistan/Iqbal: A Brave Boy from Pakistan*

Woodson, Jacqueline (illus. E. B. Lewis). *The Other Side*

Yee, Paul (illus. Shaoli Wang). *Shu-Li and Tamara* (Sequel: *Shu-Li and Diego*)

Novels

Applegate, Katherine. *Wishtree*

Bajaj, Varsha. *Count Me In*

Cartaya, Pablo. *Each Tiny Spark*

———. *Marcus Vega Doesn't Speak Spanish*

Curtis, Christopher Paul. *Bud, Not Buddy* (Also: *Elijah of Buxton, The Mighty Miss Malone, The Journey of Little Charlie*)

Ellis, Deborah. The Breadwinner (trilogy)

———. *My Name Is Parvana*

Flake, Sharon G. *The Skin I'm In*

Gino, Alex. *You Don't Know Everything, Jilly P!*

Hiranandani, Veera. *The Night Diary*

Johnson, Varian. *The Parker Inheritance*

Kadohata, Cynthia. *A Place to Belong*

———. *Kira-Kira*

Kogawa, Joy. *Naomi's Road*

Lin, Grace. *The Year of the Dog*

Medina, Meg. *Merci Suárez Changes Gears*

Moore, David Barclay. *The Stars Beneath Our Feet*

Muñoz Ryan, Pam. *Esperanza Rising*

Park, Linda Sue. *A Single Shard*

Pignat, Caroline. *The Gospel Truth*

Reynolds, Jason. *As Brave as You*

———. *Look Both Ways: A Tale Told in Ten Blocks*

———. Track series (*Ghost, Patina, Sunny, Lu*)

Rhodes, Jewell Parker. *Ghost Boys*

Rosenberg, Madelyn, and Wendy Wan-Long Shang. *This Is Just a Test*

Roy, Jennifer, with Ali Fadhil. *Playing Atari with Saddam Hussein: Based on a True Story*
Saeed, Aisha. *Amal Unbound*
Spinelli, Jerry. *Maniac Magee*
Taylor, Mildred D. *Roll of Thunder, Hear My Cry*
Weeks, Sarah, and Gita Varadarajan. *Save Me a Seat*
Woodson, Jacqueline. *Harbor Me*
Yang, Kelly. *Front Desk*

Young Adult

Ellis, Deborah, and Eric Walters. *Bifocal*
Khorram, Adib. *Darius the Great Is Not Okay*
Myers, Walter Dean. *Monster*
Schmidt, Gary D. *The Wednesday Wars* (Sequel: *Okay for Now*)
Thomas, Angie. *The Hate U Give*
Warga, Jasmine. *Other Words for Home*

Other

Hudson, Wade, and Cheryl Willis Hudson, eds. *We Rise, We Resist, We Raise Our Voices* (essays, letters, poems and stories)
Moyer, Naomi M. *Black Women Who Dared*
Sanders, Rob (illus. Jared Andrew Schorr). *Peaceful Fights for Equal Rights*
Spilsbury, Louise A. (illus. Hanane Kai). *Racism and Intolerance* (nonfiction)
Stephens, R. David, ed. *Henry Chow and Other Stories* (short stories)

"A recent survey from BookNet Canada confirmed that people actually want to buy books that reflected cultures other than their own — whether they are already considered well represented in books or not."

— Deborah Dundas, "Who Do We See in Kids' Books?" *Toronto Star*, October 25, 2019

Chapter 2

The Immigrant and Refugee Experience

*Different languages, different food, different customs.
That's our neighborhood: wild and tangled. Like the
best kind of garden.*

*A few months ago, a new family, Samar's family,
rented the blue house. They were from a distant
country. Their ways were unfamiliar. Their words
held new music.*

*Just another transplant in our messy garden, it
seemed.*

— From *Wishtree* by Katherine Applegate

*Once there was a boy who had to leave his home
. . . and find another. In his bag he carried a book, a
bottle, and a blanket.*

*In his teacup he held some earth from where he
used to play.*

— From *Teacup* by Rebecca Young

*Let me experience fully these people who are so
different from me. Let me be part of this fabric. Not
disappear into it, not become them, but be with them.*

— From *A Perfect Ganesh* by Terrence McNally

In preparing to introduce this tough topic, I came across an article titled "'One Day We Had to Run': The Development of the Refugee Identity in Children's Literature and Its Function in Education." In this article, educator Julia Hope claims that refugees in British schools are increasing and, as a result, books dealing with the struggle and survival of those who flee their countries are being published in great numbers. Hope provides an ethnography study to consider the significance of personal testimony and understanding of real historical events and fictional refugee characters in children's literature. *The Silver Sword* by Ian Serraillier (1956), *I Am David* by Anne Holm (1965), and *Number the Stars* by Lois Lowry (1989) are cited as examples of stories where young people are forced to flee their countries in wartime. Her article was written in 2008.

Today's headlines inform us that the global refugee crisis continues with more than a million migrants fleeing war in Syria, the Middle East, Africa, Asia and Eastern Europe, and Central and South America. These life stories can be considered both tough and inspirational.

Humanizing the Global Refugee Crisis

Whether from an adult's grasp of the world or a child's viewpoint, it is hard to make sense of how a refugee crisis can even occur. Would it not be better if our children didn't know about such traumatic events? The facts, however, are real and present and should not be denied. As educators we are challenged to explain and humanize the refugee crisis for young readers, especially when the curriculum is drawn from issues of identity, diversity, and the making of connections.

Literature to Raise Awareness of the Plight of Refugees

As with the discussion of each tough topic in this resource, it is important for us to turn to literature to bring authenticity, humanity, and story power to learning about the immigrant and refugee experience. Contemporary publishers recognize this essential need. From picture books to young adult titles, from fiction to nonfiction, a range of titles are currently available to advance understanding of the world of immigrants and refugees. This world, where war, natural disaster, or acts of terrorism drive families out of their home countries, is much broader in scope than in past decades.

Many students who sit in today's classrooms, urban and rural, have been part of those experiences. To build empathy and caring within our students, we must raise their awareness of people who are confronted with the desperate need to find a place of safety, a place of belonging, a place that is home in the community. For immigrant and refugee children in our midst, the school *is* that community. Raising awareness is a vital first step in understanding the backgrounds and lives of refugee children. Relevant books can also help to validate the experiences of children who have been immigrants or refugees.

Literature to Foster Safe and Welcoming Communities

According to Margaret Meek (2001, x), children's literature plays an important part "in the development of children's understanding of both belonging (being one of us) and differentiation (being other)." In a curriculum that values social justice, diversity, and equity, teachers — and their students — need to welcome immigrants, many of whom have come through extraordinary experiences and trauma. Friendship and acceptance are essential to help people of different cultural and social backgrounds find a place of belonging.

In most communities and schools today, citizens will likely have some contact with immigrants or refugees who are newly arrived into their neighborhoods. Asking questions and learning about these neighbors, who have likely left much behind, can help to uncover assumptions about and perceptions of refugees and asylum seekers. Refugee stories have the potential for challenging stereotypes and countering racism; they can help children make stronger connections with the experiences of others.

Many children encountering the strangeness of living in a new country identify with picture book characters. In *Mustafa* by Marie-Louise Gay, there is Mustafa, who strives to enjoy life in his new home while meeting the challenge of learning a new language. In *The Name Jar* by Yangsook Choi, there is Unhei, who is anxious that American kids will not like her. *Out* by Angela May George, *The Journey* by Francesca Sanna, and *The Day War Came* by Nicola Davies can open doors to understanding of refugees and migrants who have travelled from countries all over the world and can connect many students to their own experiences of leaving their homelands.

Many teachers of Grades 6 through 8 recognize the title *Refugee* by Alan Gratz as powerful and essential novel reading to help young adolescents dig into historical events framed around the stories of three refugees: a Jewish boy in Nazi Germany, a Cuban girl in 1994, and a Syrian boy in 2015. Gratz's book, along with free verse novels *Home of the Brave* by Katherine Applegate, *Inside Out & Back Again* by Thanhha Lai, and *Other Words for Home* by Jasmine Warga, would provide a strong literature base for exploring the topic.

When engaged with literature, students can begin to make sense of historical events and raise questions about the political circumstances that led to those events. Moreover, these powerful stories move beyond just giving information to arousing strong emotions. When students read about the determination and resilience of characters who are victims of political and social circumstances that have put their lives at risk, both mind and heart are engaged. Julia Hope (2008, 300) affirms, "Children's literature about the refugee experience is an ideal context for sharing stories, feelings and fears that many children have had to deal with in their relatively short lives."

Today's books may be drawn from wider global experiences than those that Hope addressed, but some universal truths apply to the narratives in past and current books. In a sense, we are *all* immigrants. Every family has a heritage story about ancestors who have moved from one country to another. It is important to have these stories revealed and to learn about the fictional and real stories of others. These stories can facilitate dialogue and foster empathy. In a diverse and equitable classroom, they can help young people accept that an immigrant or refugee can "be one of us" while holding on to their "otherness." Children's literature can inform young people about how yesterday's refugees held on to hope and showed the courage to survive and find a safe home. It can also help students to take action to ensure safe and welcoming environments in today's communities — and in those of tomorrow.

In the Perspective feature that follows, Arif Anwar reminds us that the immigrant and refugee experience is ultimately a human experience that affects all of us.

Why We Need to Teach About Immigrants and Refugees

by Arif Anwar

It is important to learn about immigrants and refugees because we might have them in our family trees or because these terms have been applied to us in the past or may be applied in the future. At the same time, words such as *immigrants* and *refugees* are labels. Calling people *immigrants* or *refugees* neither eclipses their past nor defines their future. It is only a part of their identity.

Although the topic has taken on some urgency because of Arab Spring and the Syrian Civil War, refugees have existed throughout history. Refugees are often the victims of intricately connected global economic and political alliances that prop up oppressive governments in rich and other resource-rich countries. Many are political refugees from civil strife.

Immigrants and Refugees — They Are Us

One way to understand the immigrant or refugee experience is through literature, a powerful vehicle for truth that allows us to experience the world through the senses of another. However, when you seek to understand the immigrant or refugee experience, do not simply pursue the easy path of doing a search for books that contain the terms in their descriptions; rather, seek literature grounded in the cultures — in the past and in the future of the people you wish to learn about — not merely a window in time when people are defined in relation to their legal status in a new land.

As you read these works, remember that the immigrant or refugee experience is a *human* experience. There have been times and places in all our lives where we have been the stranger, unsure of ourselves, hoping for a kind smile or a welcoming word. In short, we need to learn about immigrants and refugees — and to teach our students about them — not because they are different from us, but because they *are* us.

Arif Anwar, born in Bangladesh, has worked on issues of poverty alleviation for BRAC (Building Resources Across Communities). He is the author of the adult novel *The Storm*, which crosses continents and interconnects stories of immigration drawn from 50 years of Bangladeshi history.

The Language and Vocabulary of the Immigrant and Refugee Experience

1. Ask the students the following: "What do you think is the difference between an *immigrant* and a *refugee*? How might the experiences of an immigrant be similar to or different than that of a refugee?" After hearing a number of responses, you could share following definitions with the students to help them better understand the difference.
   - **Immigrant:** one that immigrates, such as a person who comes to a country to take up permanent residence; the term can also refer to a plant or animal that becomes established in an area where it was previously unknown.
   - **Immigration:** an act or instance of immigrating, of journeying to a country from one's native country for the purpose of permanent residence there
   - **Immigrate:** to come to another country with the intention to live there permanently
   - **Emigrate:** to leave or go from one's country to live in another
   - **Migrate:** to move between places, such as different countries; in the case of birds, for example, the movement pattern is seasonal.
   - **Refugee:** a type of immigrant individual seeking refuge or asylum, especially one who has left his or her native country and is unwilling or unable to return to it due to persecution or fear of persecution (because of race, religion, membership in a particular social group, or political opinion)
2. Ask the students: "What do you think are reasons for people to emigrate?"
   Reasons are reflected in the various government categories of immigrants. Explain to the students that there are essentially four categories:
   - **family-class immigrants** (persons closely related to Canadian residents living in Canada)
   - **economic immigrants** (skilled workers and business people)
   - **refugees** (people who are escaping persecution, torture, or cruel and unusual punishment)
   - **people in the humanitarian or other category** (people who have endured much suffering and whose lives would improve if they could immigrate)

Opening Up the Topic of the Immigrant and Refugee Experience

Three recent novels pertaining to immigrants and refugees expose racial and religious intolerance. The quotations below echo hateful words that can still heard in present-day North American society. Rejecting newcomers (or treating established citizens as if they were newcomers) is a tough topic to address in our classrooms, but literature and discussion can help students to take a moral and ethical stance to disturbing language and hateful deeds.

Present the following samples of dialogue to the students and ask, "Do you think these statements are fact or fiction? Why?"

LEAVE!
— From *Wishtree* by Katherine Applegate (page 51)

"I don't believe a word any of these people say. They need to all go back."
— From *Count Me In* by Varsha Bajaj (page 148)

"Go back to where you came from . . . We don't want you here."
— From *Other Words for Home* by Jasmine Warga (page 263)

Written Response and Discussion

Using at least one of the excerpts given above, have students complete these three sentence stems:

- When I read this excerpt, I am reminded of . . .
- When I read this excerpt, I wonder . . .
- When I read this excerpt, I predict . . .

Students can then share their written responses in small groups. Afterwards, during a whole class discussion, encourage students to share their responses by discussing these questions:

- How truthful is this statement(s) to media reports you are familiar with?
- How can a novel help you to understand different views about immigration?
- What are some connections that you as readers can make to yourselves? to others? to other books? to the world?
- How can we help or give advice to those who make such hateful statements?

Graphic Organizers Based on a Picture Book

- *The K-W-L Chart.* Many educators are familiar with the teaching strategy of the K-W-L chart which is used before, during, and after teaching a new topic. Students record what they **k**now (K), what they **w**ant to know before being introduced to a text (W), and what they **l**earned (L) by the time the reading or lesson was completed. This strategy is useful for activating students' prior knowledge, for raising questions, and for identifying new content that students have learned. Here it is applied to refugees.

  Volunteers contribute ideas as the teacher records answers in the What We Know About Refugees and What We Want to Know About Refugees columns. After a read-aloud session with a picture book about immigrants and refugees (see the list on pages 50 and 51), the teacher can then record ideas in the What We Learned column.

If students add a third column where they list facts they learned about refugees, they will have transformed a T-chart into a K-W-L chart.

- *Use of a T-chart.* An alternative is for students to work in small groups to address these two headings after they have heard an appropriate picture book:

What We Know About Refugees   Questions We Have About Refugees

Each group can then meet with another group to share and compare answers, **or** one group can share their T-chart notes with the whole class as the basis of a master chart. Students from other groups can report items that they think should be added.

As the theme of refugees is explored over time, students can add to the list of facts they learn about immigrants and refugees through media, picture books, novels, and the Internet.

As an introduction to the topic of refugees, the students in Rachael Stein's Grade 7 class worked in groups of three or four to list facts and questions they had about refugees. Groups then shared their responses with the whole class. The following lists were compiled on the whiteboard.

What We Know About Refugees	Questions We Have About Refugees
Most refugees come from countries that are at war or face terrorism.	What is the difference between a refugee and an immigrant?
Refugees can be different ages, both male and female, and different races.	What is a refugee camp?
There are camps set up to help refugees survive once they leave their country.	How can refugees possibly afford basic needs? What if they have no money?
There are over 20 million refugees in the world today.	What role does the government play in admitting refugees to a country?
Not all countries open their arms and welcome refugees.	What does "seeking asylum" mean?
It takes a long time for a refugee to become a citizen of a country.	Where do most refugees come from today?
Refugee children can be split up from their parents.	Why would a country turn refugees away? What happens to them?
Sometimes refugees pay smugglers to get them into a country.	When children are separated from their parents, how can they find them again?
A refugee is a person, like you or me.	Who helps refugees once they settle into a community? How are they helped?
A refugee's top wish is freedom.	Why do some people seem to hate refugees?

Model Lesson 1: Exploring a Picture Book Through Tableaux

Featured Text: The Day War Came *by Nicola Davies, illustrated by Rebecca Cobb*

This lesson works well for students in Grades 3 to 9.

British author Nicola Davies created the poem "The Day War Came" in response to children utterly alone in the world and the U.K. government vote against the nation accepting 3000 unaccompanied child refugees from Syria. The poem, first published on *The Guardian* newspaper's website on April 28, 2016, has also been transformed into a picture book.

See the boxed list titled "More Picture Books with Strong Narratives for Exploring Tableaux" for other picture books especially appropriate for tableaux making.

What inspired Davies to write the poem was the story about a refugee child being refused entry to a school because there wasn't a chair for her to sit on. In the days that followed publication of the poem, hundreds and hundreds of people posted images of empty chairs with the hashtag #3000chairs. These images served as symbols of solidarity with young people who had lost everything and had nowhere to go.

Tableaux: A Way to Convey Dramatic Human Moments

A tableau depicts a moment in time, such as the arrival of immigrants on the pier. Students can represent a story by creating still images, or frozen pictures, in different periods of time depicting characters from the story or implied characters that connect to the story. Presenting a series of tableaux is a convenient way to retell story events: three to five images can be used to represent the beginning, middle, climax, and ending of the story. When instructed to depict scenes that might not be in the story, students are moving beyond retelling by considering possibilities and abstract ideas inherent in the story. Since creating tableaux encourages — indeed, requires — students to represent ideas nonverbally, this dramatic form helps students succinctly convey explicit and implicit events.

Tableaux is a meaningful strategy for retelling events from a picture book and exploring possible situations implied by the narrative. Several picture books on the topic of immigration and refugees can be used as sources for facilitating active responses to the narrative. The books identified in the text box below have strong narratives related to the theme (see also Great Books for a Tough Topic on pages 50 and 51). Students work in groups of three to five to explore the story. Each participant becomes a member of the tableau by representing a character; an object, such as a tree; or perhaps a concept, such as loneliness, connected to the story.

More Picture Books with Strong Narratives for Exploring Tableaux

- *My Beautiful Birds* by Suzanne Del Rizzo
- *Stepping Stones: A Refugee Family's Journey* by Margriet Ruurs
- *Adrift at Sea: A Vietnamese Boy's Story of Survival* by Marsha Forchuk Skrypuch with Tuan Ho (illus. Brian Deines)
- *Teacup* by Rebecca Young (illus. Matt Ottley)

The following outline provides possibilities for exploring the dramatic technique with a picture book that has been read aloud to the students.

Working Inside and Outside the Story

1. *Sequencing the Story.* Direct students in their groups to create three tableaux: one representing the beginning; one, the middle; and the third, the end of the story. This activity allows students to retell main ideas from the story.
2. *Digging Deeper into Important Moments — Exploring Cause and Effect.* Ask students to examine significant moments in this story by creating three more frozen images. Invite them to (1) highlight the climax, or turning point, of the story; (2) consider what happened before that moment — the cause; and (3) consider what happened after that moment — the effect.
   - Tableau 1: Groups choose one moment from the story that they think is the most interesting or the most important. Students create a tableau that represents that moment.
   - Tableau 2: Students create a tableau that represents a moment or an episode that happened *before* the first key tableau.
   - Tableau 3: Students create a tableau that represents a moment or event that happened *after* the first key tableau.

Students rehearse a presentation of their important moment tableaux by presenting the images in chronological order, including a beginning, a middle, and an end. Encourage students to move from scene to scene — to make transitions — as smoothly as possible.

3. *Making Predictions.* In their groups, students create a tableau image that makes a prediction about what they think will happen in the future.

4. *Making Inferences.* Students create a scene that might not be in the story but could have been. What might the character be thinking about or dreaming?

5. *Sharing a Tableaux Story.* Students synthesize the images from their important moment, prediction, and inference tableaux to prepare a story of five images that describe the events in this refugee family's life. A cymbal, drum, or hand clap can serve as a signal for moving from one scene to the other. Once their tableaux stories are ready, groups can share them with others.

Strategies to Extend the Lesson

Five ways to extend the lesson follow.

• *Voices in the Head*

Students can speak aloud the thoughts of the characters or objects that are represented in the tableaux. The teacher points to or signals a student to speak and the student calls out what that character might be thinking, feeling, or questioning. The teacher may call upon a student more than once, and the student can repeat the first statement or provide a new statement that represents the "voice in the head" of that character.

• *Improvisation*

Students are invited to bring one of the scenes to life by speaking and adding gesture or movement. The improvised scene should begin and end with a tableau image. Allow students to rehearse the scene so that they are familiar with their parts. When ready, each group can share its improvisation to determine similarities and differences to the conversations. A scene length of one minute is recommended.

• *Creating Dance Drama Dreams*

The creation of dreams is a useful strategy for digging deeper into the text and synthesizing information. Dreams can represent the dilemmas, the feelings, and the relationships of characters. When students create dreams, they can make inferences about events in the story and predictions about what might happen to the character. On the topic of immigrant and refugee experiences, dreams can be expressions of hope or fears (nightmares). Suggest that a dream sequence begin and end with a tableau. Using music as an accompaniment can enrich the presentation, perhaps conveying an atmosphere or mood for the depicted dream. Once they have rehearsed, students can present their dream sequences for others to interpret.

• *Objects of Character*

In dramatic contexts, students can pretend that they are inanimate objects. Invite students to imagine that they are an object carried by a refugee on the journey from home or perhaps left behind. Students tell a story about the refugee from the object's point of view, thus becoming "objects of character." They write the story as if they are the object. By writing in the first person, students are exploring perspective (see page 137 for more on perspective writing). When read aloud this piece of writing can serve as a monologue of the refugee experience.

• Creating an Illustration

The poem "The Day War Came" has been transformed into a picture book with powerful images. This source is ideal for students creating illustrations to accompany a verbal text. One approach is for the teacher to share aloud the text of the poem to the class; to prepare students for the art activity, the teacher invites students to visualize what they think the text is describing. As a class, students can discuss images that came to mind. They can then create pieces of art that they think could be included in a picture book version of the text. Or, if available, the teacher reads aloud the picture book version of the poem to the students, drawing attention to the powerful images presented by the artist. Students discuss which of these images they found to be the most powerful, the most surprising, and the most informative of a young refugee's activity. They are then directed to create original pieces of art that they think could have accompanied the text.

Model Lesson 2: Creating a Graphic Page

Featured Text: Escape from Syria *by Samya Kullab, illustrated by Jackie Roche and Mike Freiheit*

This lesson is recommended for students in Grades 6 to 9.

The image on page 49 is an excerpt from the graphic text *Escape from Syria*. This book is a detailed account of a young girl who narrates her family's odyssey after an air strike destroys their home. This powerful narrative, accompanied by stark images, vividly reports the destruction of Syria and the courage and bravery of those who are forced to flee in times in crisis.

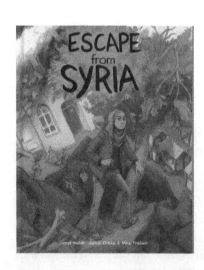

Showing a Prediction Through a Graphic Page

Students examine the graphic page, excerpted from the book *Escape from Syria*. Ask: "What information about refugees do you learn from this page? What do you imagine has happened? What do you think will happen?" Students discuss their ideas in response to the questions.

Direct students to work independently to create a graphic page that might depict this family's story at some time in the future. This scene can predict what might happen in one hour, that night, in one year, in five years, or beyond. To prepare students for their work, you could prompt them to consider these questions:

- What story do you want to tell?
- Which characters will be included?
- How many panels will be featured?
- What narrative captions (if any) will be included?
- What dialogue will be presented in the speech bubbles? in the thought bubbles?
- Will the scenes in each panel be in close-up, landscape, or panoramic view?

Some students may choose to use the comic and storyboard program Pixton *to create their graphic page on the computer.*

Once they have finished their graphic pages, invite students to meet in groups of three or four. They can compare and discuss their creations by considering the following: Which graphic text features are similar? How much information has been provided on the graphic page to tell a story about refugees?

From *Escape from Syria* by Samya Kullab, illustrated by Jackie Roche and Mike Freiheit. Printed with the permission of Firefly Books.

Telling the Story Through Tableaux

Students explore the graphic image through tableaux. The following guide provides step-by-step instruction.

1. In groups of four, students re-create the story depicted on the original graphic page by developing three tableaux images to record it. If they want, students can add narration and dialogue as presented on the page.
2. Once their first three tableaux are determined, students create a tableau that explains what happens any time before or after the events shown on this graphic page.
3. Students create a tableau to represent a panel not depicted on this page. By exploring a scene "in-between" panels, they are making inferences about what might have happened.
4. Students synthesize the five images to prepare a tableau story that describes events in this refugee family's life. Having a student call out a narrative caption that summarizes each image is a convenient way to move from still image to still image. Will there be one narrator, or will students take turns? Once they have organized their images, groups can share their tableaux stories with others.

Extension Activities

- **Improvising from Graphic Pages — A Family's Future**

Invite students to share the graphic pages they have created with one or two classmates. Group members can then collaborate to create a short improvisation of up to two minutes that tells the story of the refugee family. The dialogue presented in the speech bubbles can be spoken out loud by different characters.

- **Engaging in Research**

The book *Escape from Syria* is a significant document on the history and politics of Syria.

Encourage students to search for further information about the Syrian refugee crisis. To prepare for their inquiry, students could brainstorm questions that they have about the crisis. Students work alone or with one or two classmates to research the war in Syria and the plight of the refugees. They can report the information they learn to the whole class.

Great Books for a Tough Topic

Picture Books

From *Dreamers* by Yuyi Morales
"One day we bundled gifts in our backpack;
And crossed a bridge
Outstretched like the universe."

Choi, Yangsook. *The Name Jar*
Danticat, Edwidge (illus. Leslie Staub). *Mama's Nightingale: A Story of Immigration and Separation*
Davies, Nicola (illus. Rebecca Cobb). *The Day War Came*
Del Rizzo, Suzanne. *My Beautiful Birds*
Gay, Marie-Louise. *Mustafa*
George, Angela May (illus. Owen Swan). *Out*
Lucas, Lisa (illus. Laurie Stein). *Spectacularly Beautiful*
Morales, Yuyi. *Dreamers*
Phi, Bao (illus. Thi Bui). *A Different Pond*
Ringgold, Faith. *We Came to America*

Ruurs, Margriet (trans. Falah Raheem; illus. Nizar Ali Badr). *Stepping Stones: A Refugee Family's Journey*

Sanna, Francesca. *The Journey*

Skyrypuch, Marsha Foruchuk, with Tuan Ho (illus. Brian Deines). *Adrift at Sea: A Vietnamese Boy's Story of Survival*

Stevenson, Robin. *Ghost's Journey: A Refugee Story*

Tan, Shaun. *The Arrival*

Temple, Kate, and Jol Temple (illus. Terri Rose Baynton). *Room on Our Rock*

Trottier, Maxine (illus. Isabelle Arsenault). *Migrant*

Wild, Margaret (illus. Freya Blackwood). *The Treasure Box*

Young, Rebecca (illus. Matt Ottley). *Teacup*

Novels

Applegate, Katherine. *Home of the Brave*

Bajaj, Varsha. *Count Me In*

Burg, Ann E. *All the Broken Pieces*

Flores-Galbis, Enrique. *90 Miles to Havana*

Freeman, Ruth. *One Good Thing About America*

Gratz, Alan. *Refugee*

Kullab, Samya (illus. Jackie Roche and Mike Freiheit). *Escape from Syria*

Lai, Thanhha. *Inside Out and Back Again*

Marsh, Katherine. *Nowhere Boy*

Martínez, Oscar. *The Beast*

Park, Linda Sue. *A Long Walk to Water*

Paterson, Katherine. *The Day of the Pelican*

Rauf, Onjali. *The Boy at the Back of the Class*

Senzai, N. H. *Shooting Kabul*

Sepahban, Lois. *Paper Wishes*

Skrypuch, Marsha Forchuk. *Dance of the Banished*

Walsh, Alice. *A Long Way from Home*

Warga, Jasmine. *Other Words for Home*

Nonfiction

Borden, Louise (illus. Allan Drummond). *The Journey That Saved Curious George: The True Wartime Escape of Margret and H. A. Rey*

Clacherty, Glynis. *The Suitcases Stories: Refugee Children Reclaim Their Identities*

Eggers, David (illus. Shawn Harris). *Her Right Foot*

Ellis, Deborah. *Children of War: Voices of Iraqi Refugees*

Gravel, Elise. *What Is a Refugee?*

Hearn, Emily, and Marywinn Milne, eds. *Our New Home: Immigrant Children Speak*

Khan, Brooke. *Home of the Brave: Fifteen Immigrants Who Shaped U.S. History*

McCarney, Rosemary. *Where Will I Live?*

Naidoo, Beverley, ed. *Making It Home: Real-Life Stories from Children Forced to Flee*

Roberts, Ceri (illus. Hanane Kai). *Refugees and Migrants*

Siegel, Alisa. *My Name Is Konisola*

Yousafzai, Malala. *We Are Displaced: My Journey and Stories from Refugee Girls Around the World*

Chapter 3

Indigenous Identities

Grandma's voice shook as she softly whispered,
"Would you want to mess with a very strong, young,
green-eyed medicine woman?" I said nothing and
she added, "You are someone who can handle both
worlds — the Native and the non-Native, the old and
the new. Someone who can learn the knowledge of
the past and carry it forward to the future."

— From *Little Voice* by Ruby Slipperjack

There's a power in these lands,
One that's been here many years,
Strong enough to make you stand
And forget all your fears.
It started in the past with a blast of light and
thunder;
Ancient ones looked up and beheld the sky with
wonder.

— From *Go Show the World* by Wab Kinew, illustrated by
Joe Morse

Silent No Longer

After the performance, three seniors, Charlene, Roberta, and George, who were survivors of the Mush Hole, shared some of their stories. It was these stories that brought authenticity and powerful narratives into the trauma that emerged from being inside the government- and church-run residential school.

It was Roberta who said that work like this [*The Mush Hole*] can open "gates of understanding" to what happened. For years, survivors of residential schools were forced to remain silent about what happened. Roberta said, "I will never put my hand over my mouth again."

In October 2019, I went to see a performance of a theatrical piece called *The Mush Hole*, performed by members of Kaha-wi: Dance Theatre. This wordless performance drew upon stories and writings of survivors of the Mohawk Institute, a residential school. Through gesture and dance, strong images about what went on inside the walls of the boarding school were conveyed: a hand held over the mouth to represent silence, facial expressions of anguish, a mimed sequence of a boy being strapped, numbered red bricks that told the story of the numbers assigned to the students, replacing their names.

I did not know about the Mohawk Institute. I had never heard the term *Mush Hole*, a nickname given by Aboriginal students who were forced to eat mushy oatmeal every day. I have some knowledge of residential schools, but this information did not come from my elementary, secondary, or university education.

"The story is about hope and finding light in dark places. As much as it speaks to intergenerational trauma, it screams resilience," says Santee Smith, director and creator of the Kaha-wi: Dance Theatre.

Confronting Historical Truths

I was lucky to have attended this performance at Young People's Theatre in Toronto. Although *The Mush Hole* will continue to be performed across the country, I accept that only a few will have the good fortune to see it. I, like many around me, had a strong emotional response to this powerful piece. As an audience member, I wondered about the truths we learned and the truths that were perhaps hidden. As an educator, I wondered, what am I doing to teach students, young and old, about Indigenous culture? What could I do? What should I do?

I believe that many teachers — and I am one of them — worry about teaching this history about Indigenous peoples. Since I feel I know so little myself, I believe I might offend when I strive to build insight, understanding, and inquiry into First Nations, Métis, and Inuit (FNMI) cultures. Families who identify as Indigenous today represent just over 4 percent of the population in Canada. How can I meet the needs of all students and the demands of government expectations for changes in pedagogy while doing justice to the task? How will I deal with comments that seem stereotypical and racist when they emerge in discussions of this content?

Opening the Gates of Understanding

In the teacher education program at the Ontario Institute for Studies in Education, attention is given to teaching about Indigenous ways of life. We have an initiative titled the Deepening Knowledge Project for and about Aboriginal cultures. Each of the course instructors in the program is required to bring attention to this significant area of learning to prepare novice teachers to teach this in classrooms today and tomorrow. I wonder: What is the most important content to teach? How do these Grades 1 through 8 teachers teach their students about Indigenous culture? residential schools? reconciliation? How prepared are teachers to teach this tough topic? Which resources and strategies will open up conversations?

For any curriculum topic, teachers need to plan carefully, gather material, and ensure that they have some knowledge about the content they are presenting. Teachers may hesitate to address a tough topic because they feel unprepared to do so. But for social justice, equity, and diversity understanding, prepared we must be to educate our students about Indigenous identities. Accepting the recognition and obligation to bring the topic forward, I absolutely contend that picture books, fiction, and nonfiction selections can open a door to understanding. Children's literature is not the only thing, but it is a good place to start. Offering a range of fiction and nonfiction resources, having discussions, and encouraging curiosity, inquiry, research, and reporting are all important. This approach certainly would apply to any tough topic, but with this strand of learning, it is especially important to bring in the voices of Indigenous authors as written (for example, *Shi-shi-etko* by Nicola Campbell, *When We Were Alone* by David A. Robertson, and *Fatty Legs* by Christy Jordon-Fenton and Margaret Pokiak-Fenton).

I readily admit that an opportunity to watch a play or have survivors visit a school is not easily available to all, but we *can* bring the words from pages, illustrations from picture books, and copies of photographs into the classroom to open the "gates of understanding."

In the Perspective feature that follows, Joanne Robertson tells us how important our role can be.

The Need to Learn the Truth

by Joanne Robertson

For some Indigenous peoples, *Turtle Island* refers to the continent of North America. In oral histories, the turtle is central to the origin stories of several Algonquian and Iroquian speaking groups. A symbol of life and earth, it is seen as supporting the world and is closely associated with deep respect for the environment.

The *Sixties Scoop*, a term coined by Patrick Johnston in *Native Children and the Child Welfare System*, consisted of the "scooping" of Indigenous children from their own families on reserves and placing them out for adoption usually with middle-class Euro-Canadian families. The practice ended in the 1980s.

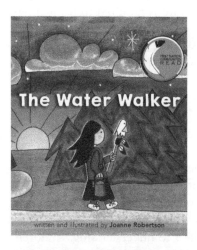

Joanne Robertson is the author and illustrator of *The Water Walker*, the inspiring story of Josephine Mandamin, a determined Ojibwe Nokomis (grandmother) who walks to raise awareness of the need to protect Nibi (water). The picture book was the winner of the 2018 First Nation Communities READ Indigenous Literature Award. Robertson is an Anishinaabekwe (an Ojibwe woman) and a member of the Atikamek-sheng Anishnawbek First Nation. She works as a research assistant at the Shingwauk Residential Schools Centre.

It's important for teachers to teach students about Indigenous cultures so that students understand that Indigenous peoples have lived on Turtle Island forever, and that if you laid it all out on a timeline, they would see we only began sharing the land with newcomers very recently.

Generations, including mine, were misled in the classroom to believe that immigrants to this land were heroic and superior and "civilized." One has only to read the comments section of media stories to know that this thinking is still alive and strong in Canada. Our Indigenous students sit beside students whose families still believe this. As teachers you need to have their back.

It is imperative that children in Canada learn the truth. Without truth, how can we possibly reconcile? Many teachers have shared with me that they feel as if they are walking on eggshells when they begin teaching about Indigenous cultures, and I get that. I was adopted as a baby and raised away from my culture, and I struggle to gain back what is my birthright. There are still many times that I feel foolish for not knowing all our traditions. Having shared that, I ask you teachers to be as tough and resilient in the classroom as our ancestors were: as tough and resilient as our children are today. You will not know everything about our cultures, no matter how many books you read . . . but still read **all** the books! It is also imperative to respectfully invite Indigenous people to your classrooms to help you. All students must know that we are not historical figures, but alive and still fighting to be recognized in Canada.

If you are an educator choosing to explore FNMI learning in your elementary classroom, know that we are diverse. Just like you wouldn't ask a student from Germany about life in Scotland, don't ask a student from one First Nation about another First Nation. We are international diverse nations.

When you talk about residential schools, the Sixties Scoop, drinking water advisories, and troubling current events, be sensitive to the fact that Indigenous students in your class may be affected by one of or all these experiences. Trust is earned.

Get to know the chiefs and Elders in the territory your school is on. Relationship building takes time — don't be in a rush. Ask them who the local heroes are. Invite them to your classroom to have these stories shared. Our children need to see their heroes celebrated among their peers.

Water Will Bring Us Together

Water is a beautiful starting point when introducing Indigenous knowledge into the classroom. There is no arguing that we all need water to live. Grandma Josephine Mandamin always used to say, "We are not related by blood, but we are related by water." Water will bring us together; it is something we can agree on.

Anishinaabe women have respected and honored water forever. Colonization and industrialization took only a couple hundred years to destroy what we protected. The climate change clock says we have 15 years to stop our negligence. It will take all of us to do this.

Learn the truth. Speak the truth. Ask for help.

The Language and Vocabulary of Indigenous Identities

With thanks to Nancy Steele and Ryan Neepin.

As teachers embark on this unit with students, it is important to explain and clarify some terms. Vocabulary words could be posted on a chart. Students can share their assumptions about the meanings of the words.

What does the word Indigenous *mean?*

There is much discussion about this. *Indigenous* specifies something or someone that is native rather than coming or being brought from elsewhere. Globally, there is no accepted definition of *indigenous peoples*. Some countries think of indigenous peoples as the people who were there at first contact. Other countries consider indigenous peoples to be the nomadic peoples of long ago. In Canada, the terms *Aboriginal* and *Indigenous* are used to encompass all indigenous peoples within the country, including First Nations, Métis, and Inuit. The word *Indian* remains a legal term in Canada: the *Indian Act*, originally passed in Parliament in 1875 and much revised since, remains a part of Canadian law.

The terminology used by indigenous peoples of the Americas to describe themselves, as well as how these peoples prefer to be referred to by others, is changing and under discussion all the time. The only consensus on naming is that most indigenous peoples prefer to be referred to by their specific nation. In the United States the preferred term seems to be *American Indian* rather than *Native American*, which has met with only partial acceptance.

Who are the Aboriginal, or Indigenous, peoples of Canada?

Both Nancy Steele and Ryan Neepin, who is Cree, have served as manager on the Deepening Knowledge Project for and about Aboriginal education, Ontario Institute for Studies in Education.

According to Canada's *Constitution Act* (1982), *Aboriginal peoples* includes First Nations, Métis, and Inuit. The initialism FNMI captures this and is now considered a legal term for describing Canadian Aboriginal peoples. *Aboriginal peoples* is considered the correct term as opposed to "the Aboriginal" or "Aboriginals" as a noun. Some First Nations prefer *not* to be called Aboriginal peoples. *First Nations* is a term used to identify as *Indian* for individuals and Indian bands.

What is meant by "residential schools"?

Residential schools were government-sponsored religious schools that were established to assimilate Indigenous children into Euro-Canadian culture. Indian residential schools operated in Canada between the 1870s and the 1990s with the last one closing in 1996.

Opening Up the Topic of Indigenous Identities

The Opening Up activities are perhaps best suited for students in Grades 6 to 9. Teachers of younger-aged students can use the line master to identify statements that they think are most appropriate for their students. They can present these statements for discussion.

The assumption statements and quotations featured on "Perspectives on Indigenous Identities," the line master on page 57, are designed to help open up the topic of Indigenous identities and culture.

Guidance on How to Interact with the Statements on Indigenous Identities

1. Some teachers may feel that they lack enough information to address all these statements. There is no need to feel burdened. The intention of this activity is to find out what the students know and what they might need to know. Teachers don't have to have all the facts about a given issue. The responses

that students make can inspire them, as well as their teachers, to find out more!

2. As students respond to these statements, they might raise questions and express curiosities about correct information on Indigenous cultures. When sharing information, some students may have doubts about what they are offering. Their wondering about what they know and what they think they know can lead to further research and reporting. For example, students may want to find out more about the water supply to Indigenous communities or identify contributions made by Indigenous people.

3. As with many of the tough topics in this book, students might reveal stereotypical thinking. These wrong assumptions can provide a meaningful context for challenging students' beliefs and educating them about pertinent issues. Listening to the viewpoints of others may bring students to new understandings.

Exploring Indigenous Voices and Perspectives

"First Nations, Métis, and Inuit peoples have concepts of rights and responsibilities based on worldviews in which everyone and everything is related."

— Canadian Museum for Human Rights
Winnipeg, Manitoba

Students can use the line master to interpret, respond to, and reflect on what the statements mean; they will also have an opportunity to share their opinions and background knowledge related to Indigenous cultures. Three ways of proceeding are outlined below.

Option #1: *Small Group Discussion.* Provide students with the line master titled "Perspectives on Indigenous Identities." Direct students to identify three statements that resonate with them by marking each with an asterisk (*). The students can then be arranged in small groups to discuss the statements and the meanings behind them. Tell them that their opinions may vary. You may want to offer the following questions to guide discussion:

- Whose perspective is represented by the statement? Give reasons for your choice.
- Do you agree or disagree with this statement? Explain.
- What questions related to this statement come to mind?

Option #2: *Independent Reflection.* An alternative way to present this activity is to cut the statements into strips and distribute one strip to each student. Working independently, students write a short reflection expressing their opinion about the statement. Students then work in pairs to discuss the statements they have been assigned. Finally, they are arranged in groups of four to share their responses.

Option #3: *Gallery Walk.* Display the statements around the room and invite students to go on a gallery walk to read them. Students can then stand by the quotation that most interests them. What questions come to mind after reading this statement? Prompt each student to record a question on a sticky note and display the students' questions on a chart.

Students can revisit this Opening Up activity after reading related children's literature, making inquiries, and doing research on Indigenous cultures. Ask: "How have your responses been challenged or confirmed? What new questions have you come up with?"

Perspectives on Indigenous Identities

I know a lot about Indigenous culture.

"People need to see and understand that Indigenous people should be considered the founding peoples of this land." (Perry Bellegarde, National Chief of the Assembly of First Nations, re-elected in 2018)

Land acknowledgments are an honest and historically accurate way to recognize the territories of place of First Nations, Métis, and Inuit peoples. It is important to make a respectful land acknowledgment at the beginning of cultural, sports, and educational events.

Indigenous people have made huge contributions to this country.

"Even though you and I are in different boats, you in your boat, and we in our canoe, we share the same river of life." (Oren Lyons, Faithkeeper of the Turtle Clan, Seneca Nations, Iroquois Confederacy)

There are Indigenous communities lacking clean drinkable water; the federal government is responsible for fixing this problem.

"The truth about stories is that that's all we are." (Thomas King, author)

It is important for residential school survivors to continue to tell their stories today, even though the events happened long ago.

The injustice of residential schools could never happen in today's world.

Indigenous people should have their own schools.

We should read stories about Indigenous people only if the stories are written by an Indigenous author.

Indigenous peoples are all the same.

I can tell a person is Indigenous by looking at them.

School is the best place to learn about Indigenous cultures.

"It must be sad for Indigenous people to have other people thinking that Christopher Columbus was a hero." (Grade 4 student)

We are all Indigenous people on this planet.

Model Lesson 1: Four-Rectangle Responses to a Picture Book

Featured Text: Stolen Words *by Melanie Florence, illustrated by Gabrielle Grimard*

This lesson works especially well for students in Grades 3 to 6.

The Four-Rectangle activity can be used with almost any picture book suggested in Teaching Tough Topics. *It is a significant strategy to promote writing and talk in response to a source.*

This lesson focuses on the picture book *Stolen Words*. A young girl comes home from school and asks her grandpa how to say something in his Cree language. Because his words were stolen from him during his life at a residential school, he tells her he cannot teach her. The granddaughter is determined to help her grandpa rediscover his language.

Making Responses in Three-Person Groups

This activity works best when students work in groups of three.

The Four-Rectangle response activity invites students to use a graphic organizer to write a response after reading or listening to a story, a poem, an article, or a media piece. By sharing their responses in small groups, students can discover whether other opinions or connections are like or different from their own. This activity is best done before a whole class discussion about the book. Once they have done the activity, however, students can turn to their written responses for a discussion where they reveal their thoughts to the whole class.

1. Students take a blank piece of paper and fold it twice to make four rectangles. They number the spaces 1, 2, 3, and 4.
2. In space 1, students write a short response to the text to consider what it reminded them of, to share their opinions, or to raise questions or puzzles.
3. Students exchange their organizers with another person in the group. Students read the response in space 1 and then react to it by writing in space 2. What did the response in space 1 encourage them to think about? Students can disagree or agree with what was written.
4. The activity is repeated. Students read both responses on the sheet they receive and write a response to them in space 3.
5. The sheet is returned to the person who wrote the first response on the page. Students read all three responses on the sheet and write a new response in space 4.
6. In their groups, students discuss the text, using their written responses to frame the discussion.

Ways to Enrich Four-Rectangle Responses

- Consider offering thinking stems, or prompts, to students to record their responses. (A list of thinking stems appears on page 31.)
- Encourage students to write their responses as if they are having a conversation, connecting to what has been shared.

- Allow three to four minutes for each written response. Doing so encourages students to fill in the space with more than one thought.
- After the group discussion, invite students to write a final reflection synthesizing the responses they have read or heard from others.

Some Grade 4 students heard the book *Stolen Words* by Melanie Florence read aloud and were guided through the Four-Rectangle activity. Here is how one group completed the activity.

1. I wonder why they took the children to the school. I hope that the words. they took away got returned to the people who lost them.

2. I'm glad the girl gave her grandpa Cree words I hope they got their words back too.

3. I honestly hope so too! Looks like its all three of us! I also hope that the cruel people stopped their cruel ways.

4. I think that there should never be residential schools ever again. I wonder why people didn't stop the cruel people.

Further Ways of Responding to *Stolen Words*

- ***Whole Class Discussion***

A more detailed guide for *Stolen Words* can be found at https://secondstorypress.ca/kids/stolen-words.

As a follow-up to the Four-Rectangle activity, a discussion with the whole class can provide a meaningful way for students to share their insights and give opinions, and to validate, question, or make connections to the insights and opinions of others. Before, during, or after the discussion, encourage students to share statements from their written sheet. Here are suggested questions for discussion with the whole group:

Glossary: Cree Vocabulary

Draw students' attention to the English translation and pronunciation of the Cree words in the story. (See the final page of the book.)

- How do we know that this young girl and her grandfather had a special relationship?
- What do you learn about Indigenous identities from this picture book?
- How do the words and pictures in this story help you to learn about residential schools?
- Which illustration do you think is the most interesting? the most powerful? (Draw students' attention to one or more illustrations and discuss what information they learn from them.)
- What are some different emotions conveyed in this story? Is there happiness? sadness? fear? love?
- How is the title *Stolen Words* appropriate for the story?
- What alternative title might you suggest for this book?

- *Making Text-to-Text Connections*

Share one or more picture books about residential schools, reviewing the definition under The Language and Vocabulary of Indigenous Identities, on page 55, if helpful. Invite students to make text-to-text connections between the picture books. These are appropriate titles:

- *Shi-shi-tko* by Nicola Campbell
- *When I Was Eight* by Christy Jordon-Fenton and Margaret Pokiak-Fenton
- *When We Were Alone* by David Robertson

Discuss these questions with the whole class: "How are the stories similar or different? What new information about Indigenous identities do we glean? What do we learn about residential schools from reading another picture book about them?"

- *Visualizing — Becoming an Illustrator*

1. Review the illustrations created by Gabrielle Grimard for *Stolen Words*. Draw students' attention to the verbal text and discuss how successfully the picture represents what has been written. ("Her glossy braids danced against her shoulders." "She touched his weathered face.")
2. Tell students to imagine that they are the illustrator for the story. They will use sentences from it as inspiration for making an illustration. Media they might use range from pencil crayons and black markers to watercolors.

- *Making Inquiry — Residential Schools*

1. Students work independently or with one or two classmates to brainstorm 6 to 10 questions about residential schools.
2. Using nonfiction resources and the Internet, students investigate and record answers to their questions.
3. In a class discussion, students share what they learned about residential schools. The teacher can record their findings on a chart.

A Personal Punch in the Gut

"When the school is on the reserve, the child lives with its parents who are savages, and though he may learn to read and write, his habits and training modes of thought are Indian. He is simply a savage who can read and write . . ."

John A. Macdonald, first prime minister of Canada, spoke these words during an 1883 House of Commons debate. When I, as an audience member, read the words projected onto the set at the start of *The Mush Hole*, I felt as if I had been punched in the gut. There was no one with whom I could share my reaction so my feelings and questions remained silent; however, our students should not be silenced when presented with such information. The classroom can be a community where students share their own punch-in-the-gut reactions, confusions, concerns, and compassion.

Model Lesson 2: From a Think-Aloud to Thoughtful Responses

Featured Text: Hiawatha and the Peacemaker *by Robbie Robertson, illustrated by David Shannon*

This lesson is recommended for students in Grades 4 to 8.

The think-aloud strategy provides an opportunity for teachers to share their own reading strategies as they read aloud and think aloud in classroom demonstrations with a common text. The primary goal of think-alouds is to invite students to notice us as readers, how we function within the culture of literacy, how we reveal our own thinking and strategies with print, and how we handle confusion when reading. When we demonstrate our own thinking out loud, we make our thinking visible to our students so they can see how a reader handles a piece of text before reading, while reading, and after reading. Ultimately, when students have opportunities to see our processes in action, they may be able to use these strategies in their own interactions with books.

Here, we are using Robbie Robertson's telling of an ancient North American Indigenous legend, *Hiawatha and the Peacemaker*, as the source. An evil chief provokes fighting among the five Haudenosaunee tribes and when Hiawatha, a brave Mohawk warrior, loses his family in battle, he seeks revenge. When the Peacemaker arrives with the desire to unite the tribes, he chooses Hiawatha to communicate his message of peace. The events outlined in this legend of how the Six Nations came to be forever altered the way the Iroquois governed themselves and can be considered a blueprint for democracy. Vivid paintings by David Shannon add to the power of the storytelling.

In the feature that follows, educational consultant Nancy Steele illuminates the connection between the legend and historic events. She also highlights the critical role that teachers can play in promoting social justice for Indigenous peoples.

How a Legend Conveys the Great Law of Peace
by Nancy Steele

Non-Indigenous teachers have been given permission and, indeed, encouraged to join in the work of reconciliation.

The Role of Non-Indigenous Teachers in the Work of Reconciliation

Many non-Indigenous teachers are worried that they do not know enough about this topic to teach it in a way that is respectful of Indigenous peoples and truthful about their histories. Rather than teach it incorrectly, they choose not to include it at all. However, the Honorable Justice Murray Sinclair, an Ojibway and former chief commissioner of the Truth and Reconciliation Commission of Canada, is very clear about the importance of teachers doing the work of ending the injustices faced by Indigenous peoples. In a speech to present and future teachers at the Ontario Institute for Studies in Education, he expressed his view that of all people, teachers can do most to change the situation of injustice that Indigenous peoples face today. He sees Indigenous and non-Indigenous people working together for understanding and social justice as the most powerful way forward.

Teachers need to learn this history, but they can do it with their students. It will involve finding sources about Indigenous cultures that are trusted by Indigenous peoples and being open to ideas and worldviews that are, perhaps, unlike their own. The story of Hiawatha and the Peacemaker is one such source.

A Legend That Dispels a Stereotype

A stereotype that has been common in the reports of European contact with the Indigenous peoples of North America since the 15th century is that European colonizers were needed to "civilize" the native "savages." *Hiawatha and the Peacemaker*, a legend based on history, challenges that stereotype. In it, Robbie Robertson tells the story of Hiawatha and the Peacemaker that he learned as a child on the reserve of his Mohawk ancestors. This story existed first as an oral history. The story of how the Great Law came to be is complicated and Robertson's book includes many of the important details. The actual Great Law of Peace, which lists all the important instructions about peace and good government, could take up to a week to recite. This system of government existed among the Haudenosaunee *before* European contact in North America.

How the Great Law of Peace Was Passed On

The Great Law sets out the processes that would enable separate Haudenosaunee nations to live peacefully with each other and to protect each other when other nations posed a threat. It also provided detailed laws that helped people live peacefully within their own nations. It was memorized by some members of each nation who, with the aid of wampum beads strung in complex patterns, would recite the laws for their communities each year. This recitation could take up to a week and was carefully supervised by Knowledge Keepers to ensure that there were no mistakes. The concepts outlined in the Great Law of Peace include the restoration of "a good mind" before decision making, circle discussions, consensus decision making, restorative justice, equal valuing of the roles of men and women, and the right of veto.

A Think-Aloud Model

The following is an outline of a think-aloud session I had with a Grade 5 class. It reflects pausing to reveal thoughts and recording ideas on sticky notes to make thoughts about what is being read explicit.

Before Reading

I have chosen this book to read today. It is a legend, which is a story that explains how something came to be. I think this story will help us learn about Indigenous tribes. I know that there are Six Nation tribes and this story is a legend that explains their beginnings. It is also a story about peace. I wonder how someone can "make peace." Why might a peacemaker call upon one Native person, Hiawatha, to help him?

I am going to write down on a sticky note what I believe this book will do. *I think this book will explain the power of one person to make peace.*

Beginning the Reading (opening pages)

At the beginning, we learn that a warrior has lost his family because of an evil chief. He is angry and thinks only of revenge. When a man arrives to meet Hiawatha, he informs him of the great law that "fighting amongst our people must stop." Hiawatha chooses to join the messenger. I notice that a message is written in large font: "And so I, Hiawatha, came to tell the story of the Great Peacemaker."

I am going to write a prediction on my Post-it note: *I think that Hiawatha will live to tell a story to his ancestors. I am optimistic that the Peacemaker will successfully achieve his goal, even though they will face many challenges.*

A song on CD by author and musician Robbie Robertson accompanies the picture book. One option is to play it to introduce the activity before students listen to the story read aloud.

I think this book will explain the power of one person to make peace

Continuing the Reading

This story describes the journey of Hiawatha and the Peacemaker. First, the Mohawk are afraid to join, because they are afraid of the powerful great chief. Assuring the Mohawk that nations can join together, Hiawatha and the Peacemaker promise to return with proof. The Cayuga agree to join them, and they travelled as one nation. I predict that there will be encounters with different councils who will each agree to join them. The sentence "Together we paddle as one nation" makes me feel optimistic.

Here is what I wrote for my prediction: *I predict that peace will be spread, but there will be some resistance.*

Hiawatha's family had been killed by the violent world, but Hiawatha explains to the Oneida about forgiveness. He says that he is able to forgive himself. I'm reminded of a time that I was very angry with a friend who talked about me behind my back. I think about the idea of forgiveness. Is it possible to forgive others? Can we forgive and forget?

I am going to share my connection on this Post-it note: *Will Hiawatha ever be able to forgive Tadodaho? Have you ever forgiven someone for what they have done to you?*

The Mohawk, Cayuga, Seneca, and Oneida tribes join together believing that there being together is more powerful. We learn that the word about the mission travelled to the evil chief, and the fighting continued. We learn that Tadodaho is very sick. My prediction was confirmed that the tribes will work together. My prediction was confirmed that they will meet trouble. I am going to record a new prediction: *Hiawatha and the Peacemaker can forgive Tadodaho and help him with his sickness . . .*

After Reading

Now that we have finished the story and jotted our thinking on sticky notes, you are going to have a chance to share your thoughts about the story. Turn and talk to a partner and share your responses. You can use the following sentence stems to guide your discussion:

- Before reading this book, I thought . . .
- At the beginning, I learned . . .
- I predicted that . . . My predictions were correct . . . were not correct . . .
- Some art images that helped me understand the story were . . .
- After reading the book, I learned . . .
- I now wonder about . . .

Response Activities with *Hiawatha and the Peacemaker*

• *What's the Message?*

1. The following words pertain to character education. Present them to the students:

forgiveness	resilience
courage	collaboration
bravery	perseverance
hope	respect
community	trust

2. Have students choose at least two words from the list and complete the following sentence stem to explain how this story validates the message:
   This story is about . . .

3. Ask students to work in groups of five or six to share their responses. (Even if some students have chosen the same word, their explanation would likely be

Teachings of the Seven Grandfathers

The Anishinaabe are culturally related Indigenous peoples within Canada and the United States. The Teachings of the Seven Grandfathers, all about human interactions, have long been part of their culture. Each teaching honors a basic virtue intrinsic to a healthy life:

Courage
Truth
Love
Respect
Humility
Wisdom
Honesty

While exploring literature on Indigenous identities, you may want to present the teachings to students both to help them understand identities and to consider an important framework for character education.

different.) Groups can review the list of words and prioritize them from most important to least important message or theme.

4. As a class discuss each of the words. Discuss how the story of Hiawatha gives evidence to each of these messages.

• *Story Mapping of a Journey*

Story mapping is a strategy that most often uses a graphic organizer to help students retell or learn the elements of a book or story. Identifying story characters, plot, setting, problem, and solution by creating a story map encourages careful reading or listening to learn details. An alternative to a graphic organizer is to have students create visual maps in an open-ended way. Doing this allows students to reveal their understanding of story elements and organize it in their own way, sequential or not.

Hiawatha and the Peacemaker is an ideal source for story mapping since it is a journey story that happens over time. Because of the length of this legend, students can work independently or with a partner, using large sheets of paper to create a story map of one part of the journey.

• *The Six Nations: Inquiry and Research*

Read the historical note that appears on the final pages of the picture book. Ask: "What do we learn about Hiawatha from this information? What do we learn about the Great Law of Peace?" Direct students to search for further information about the Six Nations Iroquois Confederacy, officially known as the *Haudenosaunee*, or People of the Long House. Students can be organized into groups, each researching and reporting information about one nation:

the Cayugas	the Senecas	the Oneidas
the Mohawks	the Onondagas	the Tuscarora

• *Sing Me the Story*

The publication of *Hiawatha and the Peacemaker* includes a CD featuring an original song written and performed by Robbie Robertson, a child of Mohawk and Cayuga descent. Robertson was the lead guitarist and main songwriter of The Band. Have the students listen to the song. Students can discuss how it summarizes and synthesizes the story learned from the picture book.

Great Books for a Tough Topic

Picture Books for Grades 1 to 3

Alexie, Sherman (illus. Yuyi Morales). *Thunder Boy Jr.*
Campbell, Nicola I. (illus. Kim LaFave) *Shi-shi-etko* (Sequel: *Shin-chi's Canoe*)
Daniel, Danielle. *Sometimes I Feel Like a Fox*
Kalluk, Celina (illus. Alexandria Neonakis). *The Sweetest Kulu*
Maillard, Kevin Noble (illus. Juana Martinez-Neal). *Fry Bread: A Native American Family Story*
Robertson, David A. (illus. Julie Flett). *When We Were Alone*
Robertson, Joanne. *The Water Walker*
———. *Nibi Is Water (Nibi Aawan Nbiish).*
Smith, Monique Gray (illus. Julie Flett). *My Heart Fills with Happiness* (in Plains Cree and English)

Graphic organizers can provide some structure for students to retell a story.
See https://storymaps.arcgis.com.

Individuals or pairs can rehearse a retelling of the story using the maps they have created as a guide to the storytelling. If students have worked on different parts of the story, the sharing can be done in sequential order with each person contributing to the narrative.

GoodMinds is a First Nations–owned family business based on the Six Nations of the Grand River (near Brantford, in Southwestern Ontario). It is a leading source for bias-free teaching and educational resources related to American Indian, First Nations, Indigenous, and Aboriginal studies.

Sorell, Traci (illus. Frané Lessac). *We Are Grateful: Otsaliheliga*
Wallace, Mary. *An Inuksuk Means Welcome*
Webstad, Phyllis (illus. Brock Nicol). *Phyllis's Orange Shirt*

Picture Books for Grades 4 to 8

Avingaq, Susan, and Maren Vsetula (illus Charlene Chua). *The Pencil*
Bouchard, David (illus. Allen Sapp). *The Song Within My Heart*
—— (illus. Allen Sapp). *Nokum Is My Teacher*
—— (art by Dennis I. Weber). *The Secret of Your Name*
—— (illus. Kristy Cameron). *We Learn from the Sun*
Bouchard, David, and Shelley Willier (paintings by Jim Poitras). *The Drum Calls Softly*
Brown, Chester. *Louis Riel: A Comic-Strip Biography*
Campbell, Nicola I. (illus. Julie Flett). *A Day with Yayah*
Dupuis, Jenny Kay, and Kathy Kacer (illus. Gillian Newland). *I Am Not a Number*
Eyvindson, Peter (illus. Sheldon Dawson). *Kookum's Red Shoes*
Florence, Melanie (illus. Gabrielle Grimard). *Stolen Words*
—— (illus. François Thisdale). *Missing Nimama*
Gale, Heather (illus. Mika Song). *Ho'onani: Hula Warrior*
Goose, Roy, and Kerry McCluskey (illus. Soyeon Kim). *Sukaq and the Raven*
Highway, Tomson (illus. John Rombough). *Caribou Song*
Jordon-Fenton, Christy, and Margaret Pokiak-Fenton (illus. Gabrielle Grimard). *When I Was Eight* (Sequel: *Not My Girl*)
Loyie, Larry, with Constance Brissenden (illus. Heather D. Holmlund). *As Long as the Rivers Flow*
Luby, Brittany (illus. Michaela Goade). *Encounter*
Robertson, Robbie (illus. David Shannon). *Hiawatha and the Peacemaker*
Simpson, Caroll. *The Salmon Twins* (Also: *The First Beaver*; *The First Mosquito*)
Sorell, Traci (illus. Weshoyot Alvitre). *At the Mountain's Base*
Sprung, Dawn (illus. Charles Bullshields). *The Legend of the Buffalo Stone*
Swamp, Chief Jake (illus. Erwin Printup Jr.). *Giving Thanks: A Native American Good Morning Message*

Novels

Currie, Susan. *The Mask That Sang*
Florence, Melanie. *He Who Dreams*
Hutchinson, Michael. *The Case of the Missing Auntie*
Slipperjack, Ruby. *Little Voice*
van Keuren, L. W. *Raven, Stay by Me*
Wagamese, Richard. *Him Standing*

Nonfiction

Beaver, Henry, and Mindy Willett (photos Tessa Macintosh). *Sharing Our Truths: Tapwe*
Charleyboy, Lisa, and Mary Beth Leatherdale, eds. *Dreaming in Indian: Contemporary Native American Voices* (YA)
Jordon-Fenton, Christy, and Margaret Pokiak-Fenton (illus. Liz Amini-Holmes). *Fatty Legs: A True Story* (Sequel: *A Stranger at Home: A True Story*)
Kinew, Wab (illus. Joe Morse). *Go Show the World: A Celebration of Indigenous Heroes*
Sigafus, Kim, and Lyle Ernst. *Wisdom from Our First Nations*
Smith, Monique Gray. *Speaking Our Truth: A Journey of Reconciliation*

Switzer, Maurice (illus. Charley Hebert). *We Are All . . . Treaty People*

Wallace, Mary. *An Inukshuk Means Welcome*

Wilson, Janet. *Shannen and the Dream for a School*

Yellowhorn, Eldon, and Kathy Lowinger. *Turtle Island: The Story of North America's First People*

Young Adult Fiction and Nonfiction

Bouchard, David (paintings by Dennis J. Weber). *Proud to Be Métis* (poetry)

Charleyboy, Lisa, and Mary Beth Leatherdale, eds. *#Not Your Princess: Voices of Native American Women*

Coates, Ken. *#IdleNoMore and the Remaking of Canada*

Dimaline, Cherie. *The Marrow Thieves*

Downie, Gord (illus. Jeff Lemire). *Secret Path* (poetry)

Loyle, Larry, with Wayne K. Spear and Constance Brissenden. *Residential Schools: With the Words and Images of Survivors*

Nelson, Colleen. *250 Hours*

Ratt, Solomon. *Wood Cree Stories*

Saigeon, Lori. *Fight for Justice*

Vermette, Katherena. A Girl Called Echo (a series of graphic novels)

White, Tara. *Where I Belong*

For further information about the Great Law of Peace, listen to Indigenous scholar Rick Hill, of Six Nations, Brantford, Ontario, telling the story (https://www.youtube.com/watch?v=0DaNMtVANsA)

or

read *The Great Law* by David Bouchard, illustrated by Raymond R. Skye.

Chapter 4

The Holocaust

It was once said that my people would be as many as the stars in the heavens. Six million of those stars fell between 1933 and 1945. Every star was one of my people whose life was savaged and whose family tree was torn apart.

    Today, my tree once again has roots.

— From *Erika's Story* by Ruth Vander Zee, illustrated by Roberto Innocenti

I keep my ideals, because in spite of everything I still believe that people are really good at heart.

— From *The Diary of a Young Girl* by Anne Frank

Let us begin by imagining a student encountering the Holocaust through children's literature and perhaps also through insidious remnants of hate. How might the historical event of the Holocaust have an impact on the student today?

Planting the Seeds for Change

Imagine a student reading historical fiction about a Jewish child who has struggled to survive under Nazi oppression, seeking a place of refuge. Perhaps the student is reading *Refugee, Daniel's Story,* or *Good-bye Marianne.* What if the reader of that book is Jewish? Catholic? Hindu? Muslim? What if the reader of that book is of German ancestry? How does the story of a Jewish quest for refuge connect to the student's religion and culture?

Imagine a student reading *The Boy in the Striped Pajamas,* the story of a German boy, Bruno, whose father has been assigned the role of commandant of a concentration camp. Bruno is unaware of what is happening in Germany. When he encounters a boy of the same age on the other side of a barbed-wire fence near his new home, he is awakened to the political circumstances and begins to question the motives that drive people to do evil deeds. Will the reader understand the irony of Bruno's circumstances? Will the reader feel as much empathy for the German boy as for the boy in the striped pajamas in the camp?

Imagine a student, Jewish or not, who is walking in his neighborhood and sees graffiti of a swastika scrawled on a wall near his home. Does that child understand why this is a hate crime? Can the child begin to grasp where this hate has come from?

Children's Literature as a Stepping-Stone

Studying the Holocaust can help students to understand the roots of prejudice, racism, and stereotyping. When students read or listen to stories about the Holocaust, they may begin to grasp the horrors of war, the dangers of dictatorship, and the politics of religious intolerance. Children's literature can take students to other times and other places, and when the characters and settings are drawn from historical events, readers are mining narratives where facts and fiction merge. Reading or listening to picture books, fiction, and nonfiction texts can be a stepping-stone into learning about the Holocaust, and this learning can open students' minds and hearts to the harsh facts of religious intolerance and genocide.

An Awareness of Complexity

Many students in today's schools may have limited knowledge or awareness of the Holocaust. If young people have not yet encountered media and texts about the killing of six million Jews, then schools are likely the forum for introducing the tough topic. But teachers may wonder: What age is too young? What information can the students grasp at different developmental stages and grade levels? What information is enough? What information is too much?

As with other tough topics, teaching Holocaust history demands strong sensitivity and acute awareness of the complexity connected to the content. As with other tough topics, too, a children's literature title can open doors to learning about and understanding the topic. The fear of not having enough information may, however, discourage some teachers from embarking on the topic. It need not. Teachers are not obliged to have all the answers to students' questions, but they should be prepared for questions to be revealed and subsequently researched.

The Pivotal Role of the Classroom

"Those who cannot remember the past are condemned to repeat it."

— George Santayana

"Be the change that you wish to see in the world."

— Mahatma Gandhi

Introducing this tough topic connects students to the past and the present, encouraging them to contemplate their own role in creating inclusion and harmony. In this way, Holocaust education can help students to develop their social awareness and understanding of social justice, diversity, and equity. Exposing elementary students to this period in history is important because it will help make them aware of antisemitism and other forms of bigotry that mar our world.

The classroom can plant the seeds for possible change. *The Boy in the Striped Pajamas* (historical fiction), *The Diary of a Young Girl* (nonfiction), *White Bird* (graphic text), *The Promise* (picture book), and many titles by Kathy Kacer are examples of literature that can fuel the readers in our classrooms to discuss and investigate this period in history. Moreover, they can, perhaps, come to believe that "in spite of everything . . . people are really good at heart."

The Perspective feature by Kathy Kacer addresses some of the uncertainties about how and when to introduce students to the Holocaust.

How to Teach About the Holocaust

by Kathy Kacer

I have written more than 20 books that focus on stories of the Holocaust. As a child of Holocaust survivors, I feel a personal responsibility to collect these stories and pass them on to the next generation. But whether you have a personal connection to this history or not, I also believe that we all share a collective responsibility to ensure that this history is not lost. Young people need to learn about this important time. And there are some principles to keep in mind when working with this difficult topic in the classroom.

1. *Be sensitive to the age and stage of development of the young people who are learning this history.* We know that information that is too graphic, too soon, will deter young people from wanting to seek out more information later. And after all, we want them to *want* to learn more about this history as they mature. It's okay for young people to be moved by this history; it's okay for them to be saddened by this history. What we don't want is for young people to be traumatized by this history.
2. *Tell one story at a time.* The notion of six million Jews (and millions of others) dying or being killed in the Holocaust is overwhelming — and it's a statistic that is meaningless to young people. If young people are to make a meaningful connection to this history and to relate to it, we need to tell individual stories, one story at a time. We need to elevate this history from the millions to the individuals.
3. *Link the Holocaust to other genocides.* One of the ways we make the Holocaust relevant today is by linking it to other tragic events that are unfolding in the world: events like the persecution of Rohingya Muslims of Myanmar and the killings in South Sudan, Syria, and Darfur. The Holocaust is one of the most documented genocides in history and there is so much we can learn about concepts such as propaganda, how leaders come to power, how power is exploited, and so on by using the Holocaust as a prime example.
4. *Recognize the rescuers* — people who stood apart from the crowd and demonstrated moral courage and good citizenship at a dangerous time in history. Some are famous; some are remarkable for the fact that they were so ordinary. As young people struggle to understand this history, and struggle with how they can make a difference in their own communities, they can look to these role models — these heroic rescuers — to inspire them. By learning about the Holocaust, students can ask themselves how they can speak up when injustice occurs in their communities and make a commitment to action.

Holocaust Remembrance Books by Kathy Kacer

The Brave Princess and Me (picture book, illus. Juliana Kolesova)
Broken Strings (with Eric Walters)
Clara's War
Hiding Edith
The Magician of Auschwitz (picture book, illus. Gillian Newland)
The Secret of Gabi's Dresser
Shanghai Escape
To Hope and Back: The Journey of the St. Louis

Remembering Is Honoring

I am a passionate advocate for stories about the Holocaust. I think that the lessons we can learn — lessons about hatred and power, but also lessons about compassion, strength, and selflessness — are lessons for the ages. Remember this: Every time you remember this history, and every time you talk about it, you are honoring someone who lived and possibly perished during that time. You are giving meaning to their lives. And that is a remarkable thing.

The Language and Vocabulary of the Holocaust

Holocaust is far more than a word; knowing something of what it signifies is a start to considering the event. Explain to the students the meaning behind each of the terms connected to the topic. As the words are discussed, students can share what they think they know or raise questions about the words.

Holocaust: destruction or slaughter on a mass scale. What is now known as "the Holocaust" occurred between 1941 and 1945 when more than six million Jews and other persecuted groups were murdered in concentration camps under the Nazi German regime.

Nazis: members of the National Socialist German Workers' Party which controlled Germany from 1933 to 1945 under Adolf Hitler. The Party advocated for territorial expansion and antisemitism. Hitler's followers also believed that the Aryan race was a distinct Caucasian group deemed to be superior over other races, including Jews and Gypsies. Nazism led directly to the Second World War and the Holocaust.

Concentration Camps: death camps established by the Nazis for the sole purpose of killing Jews and other "undesirables." The major camps were Auschwitz and Treblinka in German-occupied Poland and Dachau and Belsen within Germany.

Antisemitism: a perception of Jews which may be expressed as hatred towards them.

Speaking Out Against Antisemitism

As a Canadian human rights group, FAST (Fighting Antisemitism Together) offers a free online teaching resource titled *Choose Your Voice*. The goal of the award-winning resource is to empower students to speak out against racism, antisemitism, and all intolerance. There are four units, each supported by an inspirational video, fact sheets, recommended booklists, rubrics, graphic organizers and assessments. Lesson plans include Bursting the Voice of Stereotyping (Unit 1), Voices from the Past (Unit 2), Voices from the Present (Unit 3), and Choose Your Voice (Unit 4), which prompts students to "choose their own voices" to tackle the issue of exclusion.

Choose Your Voice exposes students to diverse cultures and the experiences of different racial and ethnic groups, helping them to understand points of view different from their own. The resource, intended for students in Grades 6, 7, and 8, provides students with first-hand accounts of discrimination and the activities are designed to help them "walk in the shoes of others." As students learn about the history and struggles of different individuals and groups living in Canada, they make connections between historical events such as the Holocaust and the intolerance and discrimination happening around the world.

FAST also provides an excellent online resource to address social justice, equity, and diversity issues. *Voices into Action* provides the facts, insights, and means to enable students to act against intolerance, indifference, and hate.

Opening Up the Topic of the Holocaust

The mind mapping strategy, a form of semantic mapping, can be used in any grade to consider prior knowledge of a topic or provide a way for students to synthesize information that they have learned, perhaps through research or literature.

Students can engage in mind mapping, a strategy that encourages them to consider a word or concept and its relation to other words and ideas. As they record words and connections related to the Holocaust, they are thereby given an opportunity to reveal what they know or wonder about the people and events of the Holocaust.

Part A: What Do We Know About the Holocaust?

Students work in groups of three or four to create a mind web that will help them to reveal information about the topic of the Holocaust. Provide each group with a large sheet of chart paper and markers for students to record their ideas. In the centre of the web, students write the words *The Holocaust*. Students create five branching stems, each with a label: *Who? What? Where? When? Why?* They fill in as much detail as they can for each of the branches.

Once they have completed their webs, each group designates a member to report what they know during a class discussion.

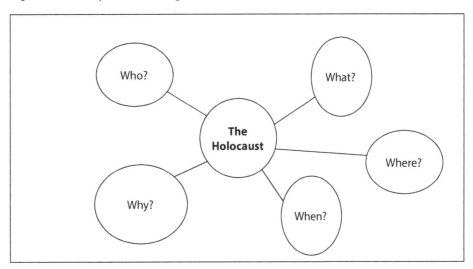

Part B: Researching Facts About the Holocaust

"Because the objective of teaching any subject is to engage the intellectual curiosity of students in order to inspire critical thought and personal growth, it is helpful to structure lessons on the Holocaust by keeping questions of rationale, or purpose, in mind."

— United States Holocaust Memorial Museum website

The activity is repeated. This time, though, the students use the Internet to gain historical facts about the Holocaust. (Wikipedia is a good place to start to find answers to Who? What? Where? When? Why?) Their work should take at least one class period.

Once groups have finished their research and included it on their webs, direct each group to meet with another group. Groups can share their information. Which items are similar or different? Encourage the groups to add facts learned from their partner groups to their webs.

Model Lesson 1: Interpreting Picture Book Visuals

This lesson is best suited for students in Grades 4 to 8.

The teacher can record the questions about *The Promise* that students volunteer to share. The students can then share their viewpoints by answering these questions collectively. Some questions may lead to further research and reporting.

Featured Text: The Promise by Pnina Bat Zvi and Margie Wolfe, illustrated by Isabelle Cardinal

This picture book tells the story, based on true events, of two sisters, Rachel and Toby, who were taken to the Auschwitz concentration camp. The narrative and strong visual images depict the constant danger the girls faced, especially when forced to separate. Three gold coins and a promise they had given to their parents keep the two sisters hopeful in their striving to survive.

Before the Reading

1. Before you read the story aloud, introduce the book by drawing attention to the cover. The following questions can guide the discussion:
   - What do you know about the two figures depicted on the cover?
   - What do you notice about the setting of the story?
   - What do you predict will happen in this story?
   - What do you think the promise might be?

   Explain to the students the meaning of the words displayed above the entrance to the concentration camp: ARBEIT MACHT FREI is a German phrase meaning "work sets you free." The slogan is known for appearing above the entrance to Auschwitz and other concentration camps.
2. Take a picture walk through *The Promise*, pausing on various illustrations and asking the students what they notice and what they wonder about. Encourage students to raise a hand to comment on what the pictures confirm about what they already know or to share new pieces of information gleaned from the images. The intent is to activate prior knowledge and determine information about the Holocaust.
3. Provide students with copies of the line master featuring an image from *The Promise*. Prompt them to complete the following three thinking stems independently: (1) I notice . . . , (2) I feel . . . , (3) I wonder . . . . Ask them to write one or two sentences that they think might accompany the image in the book.
4. As a follow-up, have students share and compare their responses in small groups. Then, prompt students, as a class, to raise questions that they might have about this Holocaust story.
5. Read the information that appears in the blurb on the inside cover of the book. Review the illustrations to determine which ones match the narrative presented in the book blurb. Invite students to predict more events that they expect to learn about in the book.

During the Reading

Pause to discuss at least three specific illustrations from the story by asking these questions:

- How does the written text match the illustration?
- What information does the illustration give that is not in the written text?
- When listening to the story, what pictures do you see in your head?

From *The Promise* by Pnina Bat Zvi and Margie Wolfe, illustrated by Isabelle Cardinal. Printed with permission.

Ways of Responding to *The Promise*

• *Responding to Illustrations*

Prompt students to identify which illustration they think is the most powerful. Encourage students to give reasons for their choices. Ask them which illustration they might choose as an alternative to the one presented on the cover of the book. Why would they do so?

• *Becoming an Illustrator*

Suggest to students that five or more illustrations created for this picture book were not included. Invite them to become illustrators for *The Promise* and create a picture that might have been included in the book. To prepare students for the activity, encourage them to choose a piece of text that might be accompanied by a picture.

• *Identifying Facts — Concentration Camps*

Students work in pairs to list five or six things they learned about concentration camps from *The Promise*. They are organized into groups of four or six to compare facts they have listed. Volunteers from each group can then share with the whole class the two most important facts they learned about the Holocaust from this story. To extend this activity, have the class brainstorm further questions about the Holocaust and concentration camps

• *Comparing Picture Book Information*

Several picture books about the Holocaust are based on the true experiences of those who died or survived in concentration camps. Introduce another picture book (see Great Books for a Tough Topic on page 78). Have students respond by validating information they learned about the Holocaust from *The Promise* and discussing new information they learned about the Holocaust from a different picture book.

Model Lesson 2: Raising a Range of Questions

Featured Text: All About Anne *by Menno Metselaar and Piet van Ledden, illustrated by Huck Scarry*

This lesson is recommended for students in Grades 6 to 9.

All About Anne tells Anne Frank's life story using words and a wide range of visuals that include photographs, illustrations, maps, and posters from the Anne Frank House Museum in Amsterdam. It provides historical detail about the girl behind the famous diary and the life of her family and hidden members who lived in the Secret Annex. It also answers the questions most frequently asked about Anne Frank, the persecution of the Jews, and the Second World War. Ultimately, the book raises other questions that will come to mind before, during, and after reading.

A comprehensive Teachers Guide for *All About Anne* is available on the Second Story Press website.

Some students may have read Anne Frank's diary already. Copies of *The Diary of a Young Girl* should be readily available in libraries for students to access. It is recommended that teachers feature this book in the classroom as they explore this lesson.

The activities outlined below can be explored without using *All About Anne*; however, this resource helpfully provides readers with a detailed overview of Anne Frank's life before, during, and after she and her family went into hiding. The teacher can choose to read parts of the book aloud to the students or students who are interested in gaining information about Anne Frank can read single chapters or the entire book independently.

Part A: Discussion and a Quiz

1. *Discussing Anne Frank and Her Diary.* Here are some questions to explore with the class:
   - Why do you think people around the world continue to read and be fascinated by a young adolescent girl's diary?
   - Have you read Anne Frank's diary? Do you think you might want to?
   - How is Anne Frank's diary a symbol of the Holocaust? How has this diary served as an iconic model of diary or memoir writing?
   - Why do you think it would be a good idea for people of different ages, genders, and cultures to read *The Diary of a Young Girl*?

2. *Answering Three Questions.* On the back cover of the book *All About Anne* three questions are highlighted. Display the questions on a chart or whiteboard. Clear answers to these questions will be learned as students gain information about Anne Frank or read the book *All About Anne*.

   Have students work independently to write answers to each of these questions:

   - Who betrayed Anne Frank?
   - Did the people in hiding get bored?
   - Why did Hitler hate the Jews?

   Students can then work in groups of three or four to share their responses to the questions. How were answers similar or different?

3. *Raising Questions About a Book.* After examining images from the front and back covers of *All About Anne*, students work in groups to brainstorm questions about Anne Frank that they expect will be answered in a resource about her life.

Anne Frank was a Jew. Her well-documented story of life during the Holocaust reminds readers of the importance of striving to honestly understand and value different faiths; to challenge any twisted, hurtful interpretations; and to promote tolerance and love.

Why We Need to Know What Faiths Are Really About
by Aggie Nemes

Teaching about religious differences has become an increasingly important part of a teacher's role due to two factors.

As cities become more diverse through immigration and migration, students are more likely to encounter people of different faiths. For example, Toronto, often referred to as the most multicultural city in the world, is home to 200 ethnic groups, speaking more than 140 languages.

Access to wide-ranging information on the Internet and on social media platforms requires students to be critical consumers, sifting between fact and fiction, if they are to gain an accurate understanding of various faiths. Students need to be able to discern fake news and recognize divisive politics where leaders feel that creating fear of the "other" wins them political points. They must learn to cope with and be critical of the sheer volume of information before them, and we can give them opportunities to investigate print, television, and social media sources. This exposure, particularly for students in Grade 6 and upwards, will help them appreciate the complexities of being critical of this information.

Accurate information on religious faiths is vital. Historically, twisted interpretations of religious doctrine have been used to incite wars, foment hatred, and justify the unjustifiable — atrocities, such as genocide and the Holocaust. What sets today's climate apart is the sheer volume of information through which students must sift.

Teaching Must Be Based on Love

In his autobiography, *Long Walk to Freedom*, Nelson Mandela writes: "No one is born hating another person because of the color of his skin, or his background, or his religion. People must learn to hate, and if they can learn to hate, they can be taught to love, for love comes more naturally to the human heart than its opposite." Teaching based on love, instead of hate, will help shape a future of peace and community.

What we believe is very much a part of who we are. Whether religion is a continuation of a long-held family tradition or a choice we make later in life, our faith serves as a way of seeing the world and interacting with others. All faiths answer universal questions but do it in different ways. When students learn about other faith traditions, they are encouraged to see the common threads.

For example, all faith traditions address the issue of caring for those living in poverty. One of the five pillars of Islam is *zakat*, paying a charity tax to benefit the poor. Within Christianity, Catholic social justice teachings, as an example, include the preferential option for the poor and vulnerable. In Judaism, the principle of *tzedakah*, giving to those in need, is seen as an act of justice, or the right thing to do. One of three key duties a Sikh must fulfill is *Vand Chhakna*, giving to charity and caring for others in need.

Going Beyond the Other

By explicitly making connections between religions, students can come to see themselves in others. Students who are encouraged to see similarities in faiths are more likely to be open to respecting differences. Studying sacred texts, researching key figures, visiting places of worship, and exploring traditions can open up genuine and respectful dialogue. No longer the "other," students of different faiths can live peacefully in a multi-faith global community.

Aggie Nemes is a consultant with the Toronto Catholic District School Board.

Quiz Answers: Part A

(1) *True*; (2) *True*; (3) *False* (Anne had several notebooks. Not all of them were found. She also wrote short stories and listed quotations from people she admired.)
(4) *True*; (5) *True*; (6) *False* (Anne had an older sister named Margot. She formed a romantic relationship with Peter Van Pels, whose family also lived in the Secret Annex.)
(7) *False* (On weekends, Anne was able to look out the attic window and see a large chestnut tree, the sky, and birds.)
(8) *True*; (9) *True*; (10) *False* (Anne Frank's mother, Edith, died in the Auschwitz concentration camp. Anne and Margot died of typhus in Bergen-Belsen. Otto Frank survived.

Quiz Answers: Part B

(1) *Dutch*; (2) *Kitty*; (3) *Amsterdam*;
(4) *2* years (1942–44); (5) more than *70* languages

4. *Activating Prior Knowledge Through a Quiz.* Students may or may not be familiar with the life of Anne Frank. By responding to the questions in a quiz, students will have the opportunity to identify and share information they know about her. Copies of the line master can be given to students and they can work independently or in pairs to answer each question. Encourage students to use the book *All About Anne* and the Internet to confirm facts and gain new information. Upon completion of the quiz, the answers can be taken up with the whole class.

Part B: Group Planning and Delivery of a Report

Once students are oriented to Anne Frank, divide them into groups to plan and deliver a report about her life. The resource *All About Anne* is divided into six chapters, each outlining aspects of her and her family's life before, during, and after life in the Secret Annex. If six copies of the book are available, the class can be divided into six groups, each assigned a chapter, such as "War!" or "Otto's Return and Anne's Diary (1945–)," to investigate. Each group can investigate information from verbal and visual texts that appear in the chapter. The group then prepares a report of five or six pages and shares it with others in the class or in the school community.

An alternative is for students in small groups to conduct research using a variety of sources pertaining to Anne Frank, including the Internet and print

Drawing on Prior Knowledge: A Quiz About Anne Frank

Part A: Answer the following by circling either *T* for True or *F* for False.

1. Anne Frank's first name is really Annelies.   T   F

2. Anne Frank received a diary on her 13th birthday.   T   F

3. Anne had only one notebook to record her thoughts.   T   F

4. Anne's sister, Margot, also wrote a diary.   T   F

5. The Frank family was German.   T   F

6. Anne Frank had a brother named Peter.   T   F

7. Anne was never able to look at the world outside the Secret Annex.   T   F

8. The Frank family hid in the Secret Annex because no country
   would accept Jews during the war.   T   F

9. The Annex where the family hid was above Otto Frank's factory.   T   F

10. The entire Frank family perished in a concentration camp.   T   F

Part B: Fill in the blank with the correct answer.

1. Anne Frank's diary was written in the _____ language. (*English, German, Dutch*)

2. Anne Frank named her diary _____. (*Kitty, Miepe, Friend*)

3. The Anne Frank House is in the city of _____. (*Amsterdam, Berlin, Warsaw*)

4. The residents of the Secret Annex were in hiding for _____ year(s). (*1, 2, 3*)

5. *The Diary of a Young Girl* has been translated into more than _____ languages. (*10, 70, 100*)

sources; they can then report what they learn. Each group explores a different facet of information. Suggested topics:

- Anne Frank's life before the Secret Annex
- The hidden life of the Frank family in the Secret Annex
- Other residents in the Secret Annex and their role in Anne's story
- How Anne Frank and her family came to be captured
- The fate of Anne Frank and her family after capture
- The legacy of Anne Frank: How and why a diary came to be read by millions

Part C: Generating Questions, Researching Answers

Students can work independently or in pairs to brainstorm new questions they have about Anne Frank, the experience of the family hiding, or the Holocaust. Students might use these questions to conduct further inquiry and research about the topic. Some students may wish to take advantage of the invitation given in *All About Anne* to search for answers on the Anne Frank website (www.annefrank. org) or to contact mijnvraag@annefrank.nl.

Another approach to having students plan and prepare a report is for individual students or pairs to focus on a single chapter.

An Invitation to Inquiry

From the final page of *All About Anne*:

"Everything about Anne in one book?

"Of course that's not possible. Hopefully you even have some new questions. You can often find answers on our website www. annefrank.org, or in other books about Anne Frank. You can also read *Anne Frank: The Diary of a Young Girl*, the most famous publication of Anne's diaries! If you cannot find the answer to your question anywhere, please let us know: mijnvraag@ annefrank.nl."

Further Reading About Anne Frank

Churnin, Nancy (illus. Yevgenia Nayberg). *Martin & Anne: The Kindred Spirits of Dr. Martin Luther King, Jr. and Anne Frank*

Folman, Ari (illus. David Polonsky). *Anne Frank's Diary: The Graphic Adaptation* (YA)

Frank, Anne. *The Diary of a Young Girl*

Gies, Miep. *Anne Frank Remembered: The Story of the Woman Who Helped to Hide the Frank Family*

Gold, Alison Leslie. *Memories of Anne Frank: Reflections of a Childhood Friend*

Gottesfeld, Jeff (illus. Peter McCarty). *The Tree in the Courtyard: Looking Through Anne Frank's Window* (picture book)

Miller, David Lee, and Steven Jay Rubin (illus. Elizabeth Baddeley). *The Cat Who Lived with Anne Frank* (picture book)

Van der Rol, Ruud. *Anne Frank: Beyond the Diary: A Photographic Remembrance*

Great Books for a Tough Topic

Picture Books

Bat Zvi, Pnina, and Margie Wolfe (illus. Isabelle Cardinal). *The Promise*

Bisson, Michelle (illus. El Primo Ramon). *Hedy's Journey: The True Story of a Hungarian Girl Fleeing the Holocaust*

Gallaz, Christophe (illus. Roberto Innocenti). *Rose Blanche*

Gottesfeld, Jeff (illus. Peter McCarty). *The Tree in the Courtyard: Looking Through Anne Frank's Window*

Johnston, Tony (illus. Ron Mazellan). *The Harmonica*

Lewis, J. Patrick (illus. Yevgenia Nayberg). *The Wren and the Sparrow*

Renaud, Anne (illus. Richard Rudnicki). *Fania's Heart*

Upjohn, Rebecca (illus. Renné Benoit). *The Secret of the Village Fool*

Zee, Ruth Vander (illus. Roberto Innocenti). *Erika's Story*

Historical Fiction

Arato, Rona. *The Ship to Nowhere: On Board the Exodus* (Also: *The Last Train: A Holocaust Story*)

Dauvillier, Loic. *Hidden: A Child's Story of the Holocaust*

Gleitzman, Morris. *Once* (Sequel: *Then*)

Gratz, Alan. *Refugee*

Levine, Karen. *Hana's Suitcase*

Lowry, Lois. *Number the Stars*

Matas, Carol. *Daniel's Story*

McKay, Sharon E. *The End of the Line*

Palacio, R. J. *White Bird: A Wonder Story* (graphic novel)

Watts, Irene N. (illus. Kathryn E. Shoemaker). *Good-bye Marianne: A Story of Growing Up in Nazi Germany* (graphic novel)

Yolen, Jane. *The Devil's Arithmetic*

Young Adult

Boyne, John. *The Boy in the Striped Pajamas*

Folman, Ari (illus. David Polonsky). *Anne Frank's Diary: The Graphic Adaptation*

Spinelli, Jerry. *Milkweed*

Stamper, Vesper. *What the Night Sings*

Wiseman, Eva. *Another Me*

Yolen, Jane. *Mapping the Bones*

Nonfiction

Eisen, Max. *By Chance Alone: A Remarkable True Story of Courage and Survival at Auschwitz* (YA)

Kacer, Kathy, with Jordana Lebowitz. *To Look a Nazi in the Eye: A Teen's Account of a War Criminal Trial*

Kacer, Kathy, ed. *We Are Their Voice: Young People Respond to the Holocaust*

Rubenstein, Eli, with March of the Living. *Witness: Passing the Torch of Holocaust Memory to New Generations* (YA)

Metselaar, Menno, and Piet Van Ledden. *All About Anne*

Setterington, Ken. *Branded by the Pink Triangle* (YA)

Wees, Janet. *When We Were Shadows*

Chapter 5

Physical and Mental Challenges

If I found a magic lamp and could have one wish, I would wish that I had a normal face that no one ever noticed at all. I would wish that I could walk down the street without people seeing me and then doing that look-away thing. Here's what I think: the only reason I'm not ordinary is that no one else sees me that way.

— From *Wonder* by R. J. Palacio

At school they say I'm wired bad, or wired mad, or wired sad, or wired glad, depending on my mood and what teacher has ended up with me. But there is no doubt about it. I'm wired.

— From *Joey Pigza Swallowed the Key* by Jack Gantos

Everybody is smart in different ways. But if you judge a fish by its ability to climb a tree, it will live its life believing it is stupid.

— From *Fish in a Tree* by Lynda Mullaly Hunt

We are all unique. We are all different. Our races, religious beliefs, gender identities, sexual preferences, and socio-economic statuses are dimensions that make us as different from other people as our physical features and mental abilities do.

Strengthening Inclusiveness

About 6 percent of children ages 5 to 15 have disabilities, and most of them attend our schools. Our students may know someone in their classroom, in the classroom next door, or in their school and community population who is different because of their disabilities. That unique person might even be a member of their own family.

According to the World Health Organization, about one in five people 15 years and over has had at least one disability limiting them in their daily activities; that fact likely indicates that our students know personally someone who has a common disability, perhaps physical disability, vision impairment, deafness, or autism spectrum disorder. They may thereby have an opportunity to gain an authentic understanding of what it means to be physically or mentally different.

Literature to Learn About Life with a Disability

Still, whether young people know someone who is differently abled or not, children's literature can provide significant narratives that help readers learn how characters approach life physically and emotionally day by day and, also, how others support or include — or do not support and include — them. There is much to be learned from wheelchair-bound Susan who, in *Susan Laughs*, can sing and swing and ride and get angry or sad; Cece Bell, who enters a new school with a Phonic Ear in *El Deafo*; Aven, a girl with no arms, and Connor, a boy with Tourette syndrome, in *Insignificant Events in the Life of a Cactus*; Melody, a girl with cerebral palsy, in *Out of My Mind*; and the little boy in the song/picture book *Don't Laugh at Me* who was born "a little different" and pretends it doesn't hurt when people point and stare.

What Disability Means as a Human Rights Issue

Disability is now understood as a human rights issue. *Social justice* is a way of seeing the world, interacting with people, and taking action aimed at removing barriers to equity and human rights. Social justice, freedom, and inclusion for all are priorities. *Diversity* means that every individual is unique and that individual differences are recognized.

So, our classrooms need to be places of inclusion, based on principles of acceptance, ensuring that our students with physical and mental challenges feel part of the school environment. Ensuring accessibility for these students is required by law. Providing a safe space where students are free from being taunted because of their differences complies with the principles of social justice, diversity, and equity learning.

Inclusion needs to be carefully taught.

An Outstanding Individual — A Challenge to Assumptions

Since the publication of *Wonder* by R. J. Palacio in 2012, the character August, or Auggie, Pullman has become an iconic hero. Auggie is unique not just because of the facial deformity he was born with, but for his courage, his determination, and his I-just-want-to-be-normal outlook on life. On the novel's first page, he shares a wish that he "could walk down the street without people seeing me and doing that look-away thing." At the end of the book, Auggie wins an award for displaying qualities that define us as human beings:

Kindness   **Courage**   **Friendship**   **Character**

Auggie has become the model of fictional — and real — characters who learn to embrace life and demonstrate these positive human qualities. Characters like Auggie serve to educate and invite readers to think of their own assumptions, attitudes, and behaviors when playing or working with someone who has a disability.

What Teachers Can Achieve Through This Unit

Exploring this tough topic may not give our students a complete picture of those who are physically and mentally challenged, but it will expand their picture. For example, mental challenges are not always visible to others. If, however, we provide and promote novels such as *Rules* (autism); *Joey Pigza Swallowed the Key* (ADHD), *Fish in a Tree* (learning disability), and *Some Kind of Happiness* (mental health), we can help make explicit the issue of mental health for our students.

If readers dig into a text and have opportunities to share their responses, they will, it is hoped, be conscious of not doing that "look-away thing" when encountering someone who is differently abled. If we can raise student awareness to not point and stare but to spread kindness, then our important work with social justice, diversity, and equity within this unit will have been well worth the effort.

In the feature below, John Myers takes a deeply personal perspective to discuss how experiences and views of people with physical and mental challenges have changed over time.

PERSPECTIVE

Why Addressing Physical and Mental Challenges Is Important

by John Myers

Let's start with SHAME. I felt shame at being visually impaired and diagnosed as such as an infant. This was such that there was a question as to whether I could go to regular school. Even sitting at the front of a class was no guarantee I could read what was on the chalkboard or, currently, on a PowerPoint slide. Shame at having up and down moods as has been the case in my family. Shame at having such pale sensitive skin that for months on end walking in the sunshine is a recipe for severe burns as happened in my early school days, even for periods as short as recess. So, hanging out in a park or outdoor swimming at the pool or campground was not on.

Students Can Move from Shame to Support

How many students hide their perceived weaknesses out of a sense of shame, or, as the play and movie title go, because they feel as though they are "children of a lesser god"? I knew nothing of the reasons for the above, especially the shame, until university in the 1960s where I first heard about "mental health." At the time my mother was dying of ALS, also known as Lou Gehrig's disease: a degenerative disease that usually claims its victims in about three years. While I did go to public school, graduate from university, and have a successful teaching career, the shame pops up every once in a while.

My story is not unique. In the "old days," students who struggled dropped out and either got skilled work or were never heard from or seen again. Those days are gone, and it is cheaper as well as being more ethical to support students with challenges than to toss them onto the streets.

If we accept the case for better supporting students with physical and mental challenges, then how do we do it?

Inclusiveness Benefits All Students

As a result of being involved in early experiments in inclusion in a couple of Toronto elementary schools in the 1980s and a career in which I saw or worked with students with challenges in a variety of settings, including graduate work, here is my conclusion.

Learning is a social activity so if you promote the feeling of "we belong in our classroom," you include the "tough to teach." I saw this as being evident in a few inclusive classrooms in the early 1980s as well as in extracurricular events such as sports, music, and drama. Our main pedagogical strategy to promote belonging was a form of co-operative small group learning. Such groups structure tasks so that group members must work together to achieve a common goal. The research base is rich and there are many resources that offer specifics.

The inclusive groups were structured to make the most of the talents each student brought. Oh yes, students need to know that they are valued as learners! What happened? For one thing, Grades 7 and 8 students in my classes would get essay help in the special resources room — years before, the place was called "the dummy room," where students with special needs went. It might have been thought that students with exceptionalities would produce work that was below standards; however, when tracking them in the local high school, we were surprised that their grades were not out of place with those of their peers.

For the past 20 years, John Myers has been an instructor at the Ontario Institute for Studies in Education, Toronto. There he has taught courses on assessment and effective teaching methods. He is an expert in the field of Social Studies and History.

The Language and Vocabulary of Physical and Mental Challenges

As students explore this tough topic, it is important to inform them of appropriate language use. The following outline of activities provides students with the language and vocabulary of physical and mental challenges.

1. Defining *Disability*

Ask students: "What does the word *disability* mean to you?"

Display at least one definition of the word *disability*. Students can respond by discussing how accurate they think the definitions are. Ask: "What questions come to mind after reading these definitions? What words and facts do you think need to be added to the definition to make it more complete? As an example, here is the Merriam-Webster definition of *disability*:

> A physical, mental, cognitive, or developmental condition that impairs, interferes with, or limits a person's ability to engage in certain tasks or actions or participate in typical daily activities and interactions.

Sharing the following key points will help students understand what *disability* means.

- The word *disability* can be defined as a physical or mental condition that limits a person's movements, senses, or activities.
- A disability makes it difficult or impossible for a person to walk, see, hear, speak, or learn. Some disabilities are permanent.
- A disability can be something a person was born with or it can be the result of an illness or accident.

2. Making Semantic Maps on Disability

Semantic mapping is a strategy that encourages students to consider a word or concept and its relation to other words and ideas. It can be used in any grade to consider prior knowledge of a topic or a way for students to synthesize information that they have learned, perhaps through research or literature. Here is it used to consider words and concepts related to physical and mental challenges.

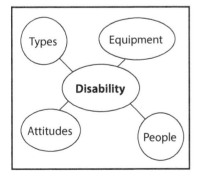

To begin, present the focus word *disability* to the students. In groups of three to five, students brainstorm any related words and connections to the word. They can list types of disabilities, famous people who had disabilities, equipment used to accommodate disabilities, challenges, and so on. If students are already familiar with semantic mapping, they can explore the use of branches that connect to the central word.

Once each group finishes a semantic map, two groups can be matched up to compare their maps. Then as a class, discuss key vocabulary connected to the word *disability*.

Be sure to draw students' attention to the word *ableism*, as well. This term refers to discrimination and social prejudice against people with disabilities or people who are perceived to have disabilities. Ableism defines people by their disabilities and considers people with disabilities as inferior to people without disabilities.

3. Choosing Appropriate Inclusive Language

Some students may include words on their maps that are not considered to be politically correct. Some words are thought to be inappropriate because they exclude, marginalize, or insult people; instead, students need to learn to choose words that are inclusive or accepted by the people described by them. Explain that it is okay to use words or phrases such "disability," "disabled," or "people with disabilities" when talking about disability issues. Provide the students with the following vocabulary and discuss why each of these terms might offend someone who has a disability.

handicapped/the handicapped	special
retarded	cripple
invalid	suffers from . . .
confined (to a wheelchair)	crazy
insane	mental

Advise students that it is better to emphasize a person's abilities, not limitations.

Opening Up the Topic of Physical and Mental Challenges

The Assumption Guide strategy is designed both to activate a reader's background knowledge before reading a text and to stimulate interest and build curiosity about a topic, which is how it is used here. A list of statements about a topic is presented for students to consider and then discuss with others. The statements are usually intended to arouse opinions, beliefs, and attitudes about the topic. Based on their experiences and assumptions, students might accept some statements as true. By being asked to circle their reaction to each statement, students are prompted to consider their own feelings and beliefs.

In this instance, use of an Assumption Guide will allow students to reflect on and articulate beliefs about physical and mental challenges.

An Assumption Guide works equally well with other tough topics, such as immigration, poverty, and gender equity.

The Assumption Guide on the next page can be reproduced and given to students. To begin, students work with the statements independently, reflecting on their opinions and beliefs. A follow-up discussion will encourage them to share their opinions and ideas; after listening to different opinions, some students may refine their understandings.

Assumption Guide: Disability

Part A: Read each statement and reflect upon it. Check whether you agree, feel unsure, or disagree.

	Agree	Unsure	Disagree
1. I can tell someone has a disability by looking at them.	☐	☐	☐
2. It is best if students with disabilities are placed in special classes.	☐	☐	☐
3. People often stare at others who have physical challenges.	☐	☐	☐
4. The word *disabled* is just a label that shouldn't be used to describe someone.	☐	☐	☐
5. I feel quite comfortable when I meet someone who has a disability.	☐	☐	☐
6. Someone who uses a cane for walking has a disability.	☐	☐	☐
7. Deaf people can enjoy going to the movies or the theatre.	☐	☐	☐
8. People in wheelchairs can play any sport.	☐	☐	☐
9. Anyone can overcome a disability — even a mental health issue — if they work hard at it.	☐	☐	☐
10. I can learn a lot about people with disabilities by reading a book in which the character is disabled.	☐	☐	☐

Part B: Complete the following sentence stems:

1. When I hear the word *disabled*, I think about . . . _____

_____

2. When I see someone who has a disability, I feel . . . _____

_____

3. When I see someone who has a disability, I wonder . . . _____

_____

Pembroke Publishers © 2020 *Teaching Tough Topics* by Larry Swartz   ISBN 978-1-55138-341-5

Model Lesson 1: Using a News Report as a Persuasive Writing Source

This lesson works well with students in Grades 3 to 8.

Provide students with a copy of the line master on page 87. Students can meet in groups to share their reaction to the story about Miles Ambridge's class picture. The following questions can guide the discussion.

It is important to note that, beyond literature, teachers can choose and use a variety of text forms, including newspaper reports, magazine articles, photographs, and YouTube pieces, to augment the picture books, novels, poetry, and nonfiction featured throughout this resource.

Discussing the News Event

- How did you feel when you read this story?
- How do you think other people felt when they read it and perhaps saw the picture? What about the teacher? the principal? a parent of one of the children? Miles?
- Why do you think the picture was taken excluding Miles from his class?
- To handle this situation favorably, what do you think the best solution would be?
- What does this story tell you about the issues that people who are physically challenged face?

Writing a Letter to the Editor

When people read stories in a newspaper or magazine, they may be motivated to write a letter to give their opinion about the event. Anyone can write a letter to the editor, expressing a point of view. Have students imagine that they have been given the opportunity to write a letter to the editor of the newspaper that reported this story. What views will they express in the letter? What advice would they give to Miles's parent? to Miles?

Model Lesson 2: Using a Novel as an Impetus for Questioning

Featured Text: Insignificant Events in the Life of a Cactus by Dusti Bowling

This lesson is recommended for students in Grades 3 to 8.

Aven, the main character of *Insignificant Events in the Life of a Cactus*, was born without arms, but that never seemed to stop her from doing almost everything. When she enters Grade 8 at a new school in Arizona, she struggles to make new friends — most children can't seem to see past her missing arms. Life changes for her when she meets a boy with a disability (Tourette syndrome).

Aven's story is a fine example of fiction that helps readers consider their assumptions and attitudes about those with a disability and raise questions about someone who has "to do things differently from other people." The excerpt on page 89, printed with permission, is from the opening two pages of the novel. It is provided here as the foundation for numerous questions.

After exploring the excerpt, students may be intrigued to read the whole novel by Dusti Bowling. Doing so will help them better understand how someone with a disability gets through insignificant events, day by day. *Momentous Events in the Life of a Cactus* is the sequel to this novel.

When questions are raised by either the teacher or students, it promotes a sense of inquiry to find out something or reveal inside-the-head thoughts and curiosities. Questions can help build wonder at the same time as they invite students to consider possibilities. When asking questions about a fictional or real character, we can learn more about that person's background, problems, motives, attitudes, feelings, and relationships with others. Questions can be revealed (1) orally when discussing a text, (2) on paper (independently or in small groups), or (3) in role in a dramatic context (e.g., interviewing characters).

The class photo that made a father cry

Don Ambridge's son Miles has spinal muscular atrophy

CBC News · Posted: Jun 16, 2013 10:12 AM PT | Last Updated: June 17, 2013

When Don Ambridge first saw his son's Grade 2 class photo, he cried.

"It broke my heart," Ambridge said in an interview with Stephen Quinn on CBC Radio One's *On the Coast*.

It was last month when Ambridge's seven-year-old son Miles came home from his New Westminster, B.C., school with the picture in his backpack.

But when Ambridge took a look, he says he was disgusted by what he saw: 22 Grade 2 students lined up neatly in three rows, their teacher standing to the left with her students, and to the far right, Miles in his wheelchair.

"He's leaning in, he wants to be included," Ambridge said.

"It's a mix of humiliation for your little guy and sadness and you know, a little bit of anger. The problem is where do you put that anger?"

Miles has spinal muscular atrophy, a genetic disease that attacks the nerve cells — called motor neurons — in his spinal cord.

Ambridge said he put the photo away and chose not to share it with his son. Instead, he penned an angry note to the class teacher.

"It basically said, 'I find this photo disgusting. Please throw it out. I don't want it in my house.' Painful, very painful. It still hurts to see it."

Ambridge said he thought the photo was dismissive and harmful, but stopped short of calling it discriminatory.

"For me, discrimination is a wilful exclusion of somebody. I don't believe that's a case here in any way, shape or form," he said.

"I think what it is, is just a circumstantial lack of awareness that resulted in a really emotionally tragic output."

Ambridge said the school responded immediately, first with a personal call from the principal and then, a plan to reshoot the class photo.

Ambridge said the original photo does not reflect how Miles is treated at school day-to-day.

"He's been wonderfully accommodated. The kids love him, he loves his peers. The staff have always been terrific with him," he said.

But he thinks the school and everyone involved can work harder to make sure Miles is included.

"Be sensitive to our differences, but don't highlight those differences, accommodate them," he said.

"I hold myself to account for making mistakes in [Miles'] daily life as well. I'm a parent. You do your best on a daily basis, but I'm not above it either."

In the original class photo, Miles is beaming, seemingly oblivious. But it's that innocence that caused Ambridge to feel even more protective of his son.

"He doesn't carry that perception of any wrongdoing or malice. He's just trying to be part of the picture and he's having a great time doing it," he said.

"I think that's part of the pain for me . . . it's just so innocent where you start thinking 'How dare you?'"

Pembroke Publishers © 2020 *Teaching Tough Topics* by Larry Swartz   ISBN 978-1-55138-341-5

Discussing Questions That Draw on Key Reading Comprehension Strategies

The questions below are intended to provide models for uncovering a range of comprehension strategies using the opening excerpt of this novel. These questions can be discussed with the whole class. Alternatively, you could direct students to answer any five questions in writing, then work in small groups to share their responses.

1. Is there someone in your family or neighborhood who has a physical disability? How would you describe this person? (*activating prior experience*)
2. What are some challenges Aven is likely to face in attending a new school as a Grade 8 student? (*making predictions*)
3. What are three things you learn about Aven from this introduction? (*determining important ideas*)
4. After reading the first sentence of this novel, what questions do you have about the story? (*questioning*)
5. How do you know that Aven has a sense of humor? (*making inferences*)
6. How do we know that Aven's mother is a caring parent? (*analyzing information*)
7. What do we learn about Aven that tells us she has a positive attitude about her physical challenges? (*synthesizing*)
8. If this story were the opening scene in a movie, what images might you expect to see? (*visualizing*)
9. The title of the book is *Insignificant Events in the Life of a Cactus*. From what we learn about Aven, how is this title an appropriate way to describe the character? Why might her life events be described as "insignificant"? (*making inferences*)
10. Rewrite this excerpt in three or four sentences. You may choose to tell the story in the third person, that is, telling about Aven). (*summarizing*)
11. How would you feel if Aven were a member of your classroom? (*making connections*)
12. How successful has Dusti Bowling been in catching your interest in the opening of the novel? (*evaluating*)

Students Using Brainstormed Questions for a Character

Writing on chart paper, students can work in groups of two or three to brainstorm 10 or more questions that they might ask Aven. Once they have done so, each group brings the list of questions brainstormed and meets with another group to compare questions. Group members respond to the questions by offering inferences of what they think happens in Aven's life or by making connections to people with disabilities that they know (or have read about).

• Interviewing Aven

The following scenario can be offered to the students: A magazine or newspaper is interested in publishing an article about young people who live with a disability. Aven has agreed to share her story. Students conduct an interview with a student in role as Aven. They work either in pairs or in small groups. Using questions from their brainstormed lists, students inquire about Aven's past and present life to help Aven make predictions about her future life in Grade 8, in high school, and as an adult.

From *Insignificant Events in the Life of a Cactus*: Excerpt
by Dusti Bowling

When I was a little, a kid pointed at me on the playground and shouted, "Her arms fell off!" Then ran away screaming in terror to his mom who had to cuddle him on her lap and rub his head for like ten minutes to get him to calm down. I think, up until then, I hadn't thought about the idea that my arms must have actually fallen off at some point in my life. I had never really thought about not having arms at all.

My missing arms weren't an issue for me or my parents. I never once heard of them say, "Oh, no, Aven can't possibly do that because that's only for armed people," or "Poor Aven is so helpless without arms," or "Maybe Aven can do that one day, you know, if she ever grows some arms." They always said things like, "You'll have to do this differently from other people, but you can manage," and "I know this is challenging. Keep trying," and "You're capable of anything, Aven."

I had never realized just how different I was until the day that horrible kid shouted about my arms having fallen off. For the first time I found myself aware of my total armlessness, and I guess I felt like I was sort of naked all of a sudden. So I, too, ran to my mom, and she scooped me up and carried me away from the park, allowing my tears and snot to soak her shirt.

Pembroke Publishers © 2020 *Teaching Tough Topics* by Larry Swartz   ISBN 978-1-55138-341-5

An alternative way to implement this activity is for you as teacher to speak in role as Aven or Aven's parent. Students, as reporters, ask questions of you to learn about Aven.

Extension: The interview activity can be repeated with a different student assuming the role of a character. This time questions can be directed to Aven's mother or father, her best friend, a teacher, or a neighbor. Students do not have to be familiar with the characters from the novel but can tell stories about Aven from different points of view.

• *Giving Advice to Aven — Email*

Tell the students to imagine that they are at the new school that Aven attends. She has been having some difficulty fitting in and being accepted by others. Using a letter or email format, students can send advice to Aven, telling her how to cope, how to get involved, and how to handle any put-downs or bullying she experiences.

• *Writing a Persuasive Letter — A Movie Pitch*

The opening excerpt of the novel might provide enough background for students to complete this activity; however, students who have read the whole novel would have more information about the plot to include in their persuasive letter to a movie producer. Tell them to write a letter explaining why they think *Insignificant Events in the Life of a Cactus* is an important story to be produced for television or movie viewing. The following questions can guide students' letter-writing:

- What might viewers learn from watching Aven's story?
- How might Aven's story help others understand people who are physically disabled?
- What scene is especially important to include in a film version of the novel?

Great Books for a Tough Topic

Picture Books

Bryant, Jennifer (illus. Boris Kulikov). *Six Dots: A Story of Young Louis Braille*
Carlson, Nancy. *Arnie and the New Kid*
Cottin, Menena, and Rosana Faria. *The Black Book of Colors*
Fleming, Virginia M. (illus. Floyd Cooper). *Be Good to Eddie Lee*
Gilmore, Rachna (illus. Gordon Sauvé). *A Screaming Kind of Day*
Hall, Michael. *Red: A Crayon's Story*
Herbauts, Anne. *What Color Is the Wind?*
Keats, Ezra Jack. *Apt. 3*
Kerbel, Deborah (illus. Lis Xu). *When Molly Drew Dogs*
Lears, Laurie (illus. Karen Ritz). *Ian's Walk: A Story About Autism*
Lyon, George Ella (illus. Lynne Avril). *The Pirate of Kindergarten*
MacLachlan, Patricia (illus. Deborah Kogan Ray). *Through Grandpa's Eyes*
Munsch, Robert (illus. Michael Martchenko). *Zoom!*
Shriver, Maria (illus. Sandra Speidel). *What's Wrong with Timmy?*
Thomas, Pat. *Don't Call Me Special: A First Look at Disability*
Tregonning, Mel. *Small Things*
Willis, Jeanne (illus. Tony Ross). *Susan Laughs*
Yolen, Jane (illus. Daniela Terrazzini). *The Seeing Stick*
Young, Ed. *Seven Blind Mice*

Novels

Arnold, Elana K. *A Boy Called Bat* / AUTISM (Sequel: *Bat and the Waiting Game*)

Bell, Cece. *El Deafo* / DEAFNESS

Benjamin, Ali. *The Thing About Jellyfish* / AUTISM

Bowling, Dusti. *Insignificant Events in the Life of a Cactus* / PHYSICALLY DISABLED/ TOURETTE SYNDROME (Sequel: *Momentous Events in the Life of a Cactus*)

Byars, Betsy. *Summer of the Swans* / MENTALLY CHALLENGED

Clements, Andrew. *Things Not Seen* / BLINDNESS

De Goldi, Kate. *The 10 P.M. Question* / MENTAL HEALTH

Draper, Sharon M. *Out of My Mind* / CEREBRAL PALSY

Emmich, Val (with Steven Levenson, Benj Pasek, and Justin Paul). *Dear Evan Hansen: The Novel* / MENTAL HEALTH

Fagan, Cary. *The Collected Works of Gretchen Oyster* / MENTAL ANXIETIES

Foster, Stewart. *Bubble* / IMMUNODEFICIENCY

Gantos, Jack. *Joey Pigza Swallowed the Key* (part of a series) / ADHD

Gino, Alex. *You Don't Know Everything, Jilly P!* / DEAFNESS

Graff, Lisa. *Lost in the Sun* / MENTAL HEALTH

Hunt, Lynda Mullaly. *Fish in a Tree* / LEARNING DISABILITY

John, Antony. *Mascot* / PHYSICALLY DISABLED

Kelly, Lynne. *Song for a Whale* / DEAFNESS

Khorram, Adib. *Darius the Great Is Not Okay* / DEPRESSION

Legrand, Claire. *Some Kind of Happiness* / MENTAL HEALTH

Lord, Cynthia. *Rules* / AUTISM

Martin, Ann M. *Rain Reign* / AUTISM

McDunn, Gillian. *Caterpillar Summer* / SPECIAL NEEDS

Melleby, Nicole. *Hurricane Season* / MENTAL DISORDER

Palacio, R. J. *Wonder* / PHYSICAL DEFORMITY — Treacher Collins syndrome

Philbrick, Rodman. *Freak the Mighty* / PHYSICALLY DISABLED; MENTALLY CHALLENGED

Porter, Pamela. *The Crazy Man* / PHYSICALLY DISABLED; MENTALLY CHALLENGED

Swartz, Elly. *Finding Perfect* / OBSESSIVE COMPULSIVE DISORDER (OCD)

Telgemeier, Raina. *Guts* (graphic novel) / MENTAL ANXIETIES

Thompson, Lisa. *The Goldfish Boy* / OBSESSIVE COMPULSIVE DISORDER (OCD)

Walters, Eric. *Rebound* / PHYSICALLY DISABLED

Chapter 6

Poverty

Every day Chloe would pass Mr. Stink and his dog in her parents' car on the way to her posh private school. Millions of thoughts and questions would swim through her head. Who was he? Why did he live on the streets? Had he ever had a home? What did his dog eat? Did he have any friends or family? If so did they know he was homeless?

— From *Mr. Stink* by David Walliams

"Sometimes when you're surrounded by dirt, CJ, you're a better witness for what's beautiful."

— From *Last Stop on Market Street* by Matt de la Peña, illustrated by Christian Robinson

We haven't always lived in a van.

That only started four months ago. BV — Before Van — we lived in a four-hundred-square-foot basement. Before that, we lived in a six-hundred-square-foot apartment. Before that, we actually owned an eight-hundred-square-foot condo.

— From *No Fixed Address* by Susin Nielsen

Teaching about poverty is not only a tough topic, but a sensitive, challenging topic. Perhaps more than other topics, it is also a tricky topic. According to statistics, one in six families lives in poverty, so within our classrooms there will be students whose life experiences are somewhat like the ones they encounter in fiction.

If we know that there are children in our classrooms whose families are living in poverty, we may feel tempted to avoid the topic — we would not want to upset those students who know that they are poor. On the other hand, effective teachers would be aware of the reality that their students are bringing into the classroom. Effective teachers would likely have some knowledge of poverty issues and society and would understand how these issues affect students' lives inside and outside the classroom. To be effective, we must know our students and build relationships with them and their families, and then we must understand the need to teach across social and cultural differences in order to make the issues and material clear and relevant.

Addressing Poverty: Five Considerations

In stretching and deepening students' understanding of social justice, diversity, and equity, the following five considerations should help give courage and confidence to teachers who choose to bring the tricky, tough topic of poverty into their classrooms:

1. *Make the topic visible.* A good book can spark a good conversation. When we teach topics such as bullying, racism, mental challenges, and poverty, we cannot plan for the stories and emotions that will be triggered by the books we use. When our students who are poor hear stories about families facing financial crises — a parent losing a job, a single parent family, a family with a large number of children, an event, such as a fire, overturning a family's world in an instant — they may realize that they are not invisible. Literature can help these students engage with others in the world who experience narratives similar to theirs. Although not all literature has a happy ending, readers — whether they live in poverty or not — can find out how characters who are poor learn to make choices, deal with setbacks and successes, and retain hope.

2. *Build empathy.* Introducing and allowing students to respond to children's literature can help students develop empathy towards those who live in poverty. Learning about circumstances that have led to families being poor will help students gain knowledge and understanding of those families, without being judgmental, it is hoped. Being poor is one topic that most students — at any age — can identify with. Understanding socio-economic challenges — why some students go hungry, why some can't afford to wear new clothes, or why some can't go on school trips — might be hard for young children to grasp, but it is an opportunity to open up the root causes of being poor. Students can empathize with those who have little choice but to live as they do.

3. *Go beyond issues of social class.* For poverty, considering social justice, diversity, and equity involves more than just digging into social class issues. Books that paint portraits of characters and settings of poverty can provide lenses for exploring the worlds of the haves and the have-nots. Attention must be given to the fact that stories about poverty can help to uncover readers' stereotypical thinking (myths about poverty that they believe to be true); raise issues of racism (certain communities associated with poverty); highlight challenges faced by most immigrants and refugees (e.g., the transitioning of newly arrived people into our communities); and even reflect the circumstances of people living with physical disabilities (e.g., how their life opportunities compare with those of other people).

4. *Make students aware that poverty and hunger are global in scope.* Regardless of the demographics that comprise any school culture, poverty and hunger are widespread across the world. We can outline the root causes of poverty in our own familiar society; however, helping students understand global hunger is more challenging. When they learn through the media, the Internet, and nonfiction about world hunger, students at different ages may feel troubled. Exposure to this issue should not be about inducing guilt, however, but about helping young people feel grateful for what they have and compassionate towards others who have less.

5. *Take the opportunity to promote kindness.* An important outgrowth of this unit might be that students decide to take action to, in some way, help poor people in the local or international community. This topic, more than others

I'd say, raises a social conscience in the young minds of the students we teach. A story that touches the heart might prompt students to fundraise by organizing a lemonade stand or bake sale; take part in a food, clothing, toy, or book drive; consider ways not to be wasteful; or share what they have with others. Exploration of this tough topic can lead students to see possibilities, to "do something" — to practise kindness.

Literature to Gain Understanding of Poverty

There is a treasury of children's literature to help uncover the wide spectrum of poverty, hunger, and homelessness. The publishing industry has come a long way since the first printing of *The Hundred Dresses* by Eleanor Estes in 1944. In that story, a Polish immigrant girl is teased for saying she has one hundred dresses every day. Now, there are stories about children who just want to be able to own something special (*Those Shoes, A Chair for My Mother, The Hard-Times Jar*). There are also stories about children coming to terms with their families' changing social status (*Yard Sale, Crenshaw*), even when it means living in a vehicle (*How to Steal a Dog, No Fixed Address*).

Homelessness is a social reality that students might encounter in their communities, and literature can help them consider the turning point whereby people are forced to survive on the streets (*The Teddy Bear, Mr. Stink, Fly Away Home*). They can also learn about the harsh realities that homeless teenagers face in notable titles such as *Maniac Magee* and *Slake's Limbo*.

Beyond fiction, there are many true stories of young people from countries around the world who have been challenged with extreme poverty and yet remain determined, hopeful, and resilient. Titles include *Hope Springs* (Kenya), *The Streets Are Free* (Venezuela), *Ada's Violin* (Paraguay), and *The Bridge Home* (India).

The feature that follows provides authoritative reinforcement of the idea that poverty is both close to home and school and a topic that allows for personal student engagement and community response.

PERSPECTIVE

Poverty: The Need for Teachers to Provide a Gentle "First View"
by Jim Giles

Poverty is a widespread issue across Canada and the world. Nearly five million people in Canada (that's 1 in 7 individuals) currently live in poverty according to the 2016 report by Campaign 2000. This includes *three million children* living in conditions of poverty (that's 1 in 5), many of whom are in our schools. The relationship between poverty and education is particularly important to educators because education plays a key role in mitigating the impact of poverty and raising economic growth.

Poverty affects both educators and students in the classroom. It is the single greatest threat to students' well-being as children may enter school with a lack of resources — for example, food security, health, clothing, and housing — and this may put social and emotional strains on them.

Recognizing and Respecting Children Who Live in Poverty

Children and their families who live in poverty need to be treated with respect and in a manner that preserves their pride and dignity. It is important for all educators to build on the strengths of students, foster hope, be sensitive and responsive to cultural heritage, and address multiple skill levels and abilities. One of the most effective ways to address poverty in public education, I believe, is to ensure that our students work with caring educators who have a deep understanding of poverty, who do not view students from a "deficit" framework but rather believe in students' potential, and who work to understand what they can do to help.

Building Empathy from Inquiry

At some point, elementary students will query an educator or other adult about why some people don't have as much money as others, or why someone is sleeping on a park bench. This inquiry comes from a place of wanting to understand the situation or a desire to take action to alleviate the situation. Poverty is a complex issue that stems from a wide range of reasons and issues with long-term consequences. Without dialogue that provides insight and reflection, students may gravitate to, or perpetuate, stereotypes and misunderstandings of what it is to live in poverty. Our schools need to challenge stereotypes and promote an understanding of poverty. When children understand more about why some people live differently and gain this information from a knowledgeable adult or source, they are more likely to be feel empathy towards others.

As educators, we can provide a gentle "first view" of our world and introduce key concepts of "inequalities" and "inequities" by discussing stories about famine and war and raising the awareness and understanding of the plight of others in our world. Older students should have opportunities to question how and why Indigenous people, people living with disabilities, single parent families, elderly individuals, and racialized people, including immigrants and refugees, are more susceptible to poverty than others.

Providing Experiences Where Kindness Is Valued

We can assist all students in our schools to critically think about their "wants" versus their "needs." As educators, we can model how we value food, water, access to health care and education, and provide local educational experiences like visiting a shelter or food bank, so that our students learn that food and shelter are not a daily experience for all. We can provide powerful educational experiences with elders, younger students, and the local community, where kindness, empathy, and generosity towards others are valued and emphasized. We need to equip all students with the dispositions and the knowledge that they require in order to thrive in a changing and challenging world: a world where they can contribute in a positive way socially and culturally, regardless of their economic status.

Jim Giles is an educational consultant and former manager of the multi-year Poverty and Education project of the Elementary Teachers' Federation of Ontario.

The Language and Vocabulary of Poverty

To teach students about poverty, teachers must be able to distinguish between "being poor" and "living in poverty," as explained below. This question can also be asked of students. As students explore this unit, it is important for them to have their assumptions challenged and to reach an accurate understanding of what is meant by *poverty*.

What is the difference between "being poor" and "living in poverty"?
Being poor is related to poverty but it is different and much more than just a person's dearth of finances. *Being poor* is a descriptive phrase meaning to lack something like money or quality of life; it can be a transient condition, unlike absolute poverty as experienced in the world's poorest countries. People who live in *absolute* poverty are lacking in quality of life and are subject to inadequate food, education, health care, and employment.

Choice of Words Matters

Possibilities: Addressing Poverty in Elementary Schools is a comprehensive teacher resource by Charmain Brown and Jim Giles. It is designed not only to encourage educators to understand tensions, assumptions, and biases they may unknowingly hold about poverty but also to help students take action.

Some research about language is distilled from John McKendrick, *Writing and Talking About Poverty*, Briefing Paper 26 (published by the Scottish Government in January 2011), page 7.

In *Possibilities: Addressing Poverty in Elementary Schools*, attention is given to the language we use when opening up the tough topic of poverty. The resource cites Dr. John McKendrick, of the Institute of Society and Social Justice, who recommends that a starting point for educators is to recognize that language matters and to avoid the pitfalls of creating a feeling of them and us, portraying an undeserving poor, or feeding inadvertently into any stigma to do with poverty. "Our choice of language can also serve to reinforcing distance or to build bridges and alliances with people experiencing poverty," he wrote in a 2011 briefing paper. The language we use should emphasize that the problem is the *condition* of poverty, rather than the *people* who experience poverty.

To help students consider vocabulary related to poverty, ask: "What words come to mind when you hear the word *poverty*?" Record the words as students volunteer answers, even though some words may seem derogatory. Words may include *poor, hungry, lazy, dirty, beggars*. Perhaps you will hear or can suggest language that is more respectful and progressive, too, for example, "people experiencing poverty," "homelessness," "high-priority neighborhoods" and "low income living."

Once the list is completed, review it with the students and ask them to identify any words that seem to be derogatory — put-downs that make fun of peoples' circumstances. These words can be underlined. Be sure to emphasize the importance of students using respectful, effective, and sensitive language when speaking about people in poverty.

Opening Up the Topic of Poverty

Students explore understandings visually and through words.

Part A: Creating a Picture of Poverty

1. Ask students to spontaneously create an illustration that they think best represents the word *poverty*. Challenge them to create their drawings within a 10-minute time limit.
2. Choose one or two examples of students' work and show them to the class. Ask the students to respond to each of the images using these questions to guide the discussion:
   • What is being represented in this picture?
   • What is not being represented?
   • How does this image make you feel?
   • What questions come to mind when you inspect this illustration?
3. Invite students to work in groups of four. Prompt them to exchange drawings and consider what message the picture conveyed about poverty. Have each student in turn share interpretations of the drawing received.

A Grade 3 student's interpretation of poverty

Part B: Writing a Definition of the Word *Poverty*

The definition activity can be adapted to open up other themes connected to social justice, diversity, and equity. For example, students could be asked to define any of these words: *bully, racism, gender, tolerance,* and *equity*.

This activity provides students with an opportunity to reveal their assumptions and explore vocabulary connected to the topic. By putting students in the role of dictionary editors to define *poverty*, it prompts them to choose words that they think are relevant and challenges them to articulate the characteristics and events associated with those who live in poverty.

The following provides an outline of activities that guided a group of Grade 5 students through the process of defining *poverty*. Students worked independently, in pairs, in small groups, and as a whole class.

1. Introduce the activity. Say to the students: "A new dictionary is about to be published but the word *poverty* has yet to be defined. As dictionary editors, you have been called upon for input."
2. To begin, students work independently. Each student is given a file card on which to write a personal definition of the word *poverty*. No restrictions to word count apply. Encourage students to use words to describe poverty. Some may choose to include examples of poverty to help support their definition.
3. Students work in pairs to exchange definitions. Ask: "What words or phrases from your partner's definition do you think you'd like to borrow to include in a definition of poverty?" Suggestions of words or phrases could be recorded on a chart displayed to the whole group.
4. Pairs work together to synthesize definitions. Encourage students to include words from each partner's definition as well as add new words or phrases of choice.
5. Partners are matched up with others to share definitions. In groups of four, students collaborate on a definition. A further challenge is presented to the students by insisting that the new collaborative definition be exactly 25 words (or a word count of your choice). Once definitions are completed, one member of each group shares the definition with the whole class.
6. A shared writing activity with the students is implemented to arrive at a class definition of the word *poverty*. Each suggestion that is offered is recorded. The definition is revised and edited as the composing process unfolds.

Extensions

- Students can examine definitions from a dictionary or the Internet to compare with their own.

The World Bank Group is committed to fighting poverty in all its dimensions. Their mission statement is "Our Dream is a World Free of Poverty," carved in stone at their headquarters in Washington, D.C.

- This 2011 World Bank definition of poverty appears in the resource *Possibilities: Addressing Poverty in Elementary Schools*. Share it with students:

> Poverty is pronounced deprivation in well-being and compromises many dimensions. It includes low incomes and the inability to acquire the basic goods and services necessary for survival with dignity. Poverty also encompasses low levels of health and education, poor access to clean water and sanitation, inadequate physical security, lack of voice, and insufficient capacity and opportunity to better one's life.

Ask the students to assess the definition:
> What words in this definition are similar to your personal definitions?
> Do you think this definition is comprehensive? Why?
> What might be altered or added?

Before reading the picture book *Those Shoes* aloud to the class, Grade 3 teacher Laura Conway invited her students to create a definition of the word *poverty* that might appear in a dictionary. Students then created illustrations representing their ideas of what it means to be poor.

"Poverty is when you don't have any food or shelter and you need to find a place to live."

"Poverty is a kind of diversity. Poverty is someone who may be different from you if they don't have a house or food."

"I think poverty means, well, something to do with being poor, but my guess is it means homeless, or they have no job."

"Poverty is when you need help to get things that you need to live."

"Poverty is when someone spends all their money and tries to get money from other people."

"Poverty is when you are very very very poor."

Model Lesson 1: Telling the Story from Third Person to First

Featured Text: Those Shoes *by Maribeth Boelts, illustrated by Noah Z. Jones*

This lesson is recommended especially for students in Grades 1 to 4.

Storytelling increases students' mastery of language, showing them how words can be manipulated to make meaning and internalize the language structures and styles. It develops the ability to turn narration into dialogue and dialogue into narration. Storytelling can serve as a review for what has taken place in a text, focus details, reveal an unexplained idea in a story, and be a way to build understanding of role.

Stories, both in and out of role, encourage students to dig into their own knapsacks of personal narratives as well as create stories of fictional characters. Telling stories, listening to stories, and dramatizing stories are significant modes for revealing understanding to others and can be at the heart of building community in the classroom.

This lesson is based on use of a picture book. In *Those Shoes*, all that Jeremy wants is a new pair of shoes. Everyone at school seems to be wearing black high-tops with two white stripes, and Jeremy dreams of owning a pair. His grandma, however, tells her grandson that they don't have any room for want — just need — and what Jeremy *needs* are new warm winter boots.

Telling a Story — My Favorite Piece of Clothing

Those Shoes describes one boy's fascination with a pair of shoes he dreams of owning. Students can work in small groups to share stories about favorite articles of clothing that are or have been important to them. The following questions can guide group discussions:

- Why is this piece of clothing important to you?

- What is unique about it?
- If lost, how might you describe this piece of clothing to others?

Extension

Students now meet as a whole class.

1. Invite students to share stories about favorite articles of clothing they own or have owned. Some students may choose to share stories about receiving a gift item of something to wear.
2. Volunteers can also share stories about an article of clothing they heard about from others.
3. Prompt students to write a paragraph titled "My Favorite Article of Clothing." The paragraph should describe the clothing item and explain its significance. This piece could be accompanied by an illustration.

Retelling the Book's Story in a Circle

Retelling in Third Person. After listening to the story *Those Shoes*, students are organized into small groups of three to six to retell the story. Retelling in a circle is an effective way for students to reveal what a picture book or a story that they have just heard has meant to them. No one student has the burden of the entire telling. As the story travels around the circle, each person adds as much or as little as he or she chooses. Participants can pass on the initial round or so until they become more comfortable about the storytelling. As the teacher, you have the option to signal a change in storytellers as the story continues around the circle.

Extension: Revisit the book's story and illustrations with the whole class to determine what language and which details were omitted from the circle story-telling. How was the story changed when it was told out loud?

Retelling in First Person. The activity above is repeated; however, this time the story is told in the first person from Jeremy's point of view. Each person in the group becomes Jeremy to retell the story. Encourage students to add details to make the story as believable as possible.

Interviewing and Storytelling in Role

This activity invites students to imagine that they are characters from a story and are about to be interviewed by others (e.g., the media, by a visitor, by relatives, or by acquaintances who seek information about an event). Questions asked by the interviewer prompt storytelling and serve to help clarify story details. Interviews can be experienced in pairs, in small groups, or with the whole class, with volunteers choosing to assume a role.

1. Students work in pairs to improvise a conversation between two characters from *Those Shoes*. Choices:

Jeremy and Grandma	Jeremy and Mr. Alfrey
Jeremy and Antonio	Jeremy and Allen Jacoby

To help them prepare for the interview, have students consider the following:
- Why might these two people be having a conversation?
- What questions might each of these characters ask?
- How is the topic of shoes important to the conversation?

- What stories will Jeremy tell?
- What advice would the other character give to Jeremy?

To extend their storytelling experience, you could ask students to switch roles.

2. Once students have finished their in-role interviews, interview the characters who talked with Jeremy. In this way, those students are presenting the stories to the class. What information was learned? What advice did each of these characters give Jeremy?

Persuasive Writing in Role

Students can imagine that they are Jeremy writing a persuasive letter to his grandmother to convince her why he should have those new high-top sneakers **or** that they are Grandma writing a letter to Jeremy to explain that she won't be able to buy him the high-top shoes.

Model Lesson 2: In-Role Interviews to Further Understanding

Featured Text: How to Steal a Dog *by Barbara O'Connor*

This lesson is recommended for older students (Grades 5 to 8).

Distribute copies of the line master featuring an excerpt from the novel *How to Steal a Dog*. Ask students to read it independently and then, as teacher, read the first-page text aloud as students follow along.

Responding to the Excerpt

Comparable to Barbara O'Connor's novel about living in poverty, the book *No Fixed Address* by Susin Nielsen is centred on Felix and his mother who are forced to move from place to place, while calling a van their home. Another strong novel that explores a family trapped by poverty is *Crenshaw* by Katherine Applegate.

A Language and Drama unit on the topic of being homeless is outlined in *Dramathemes*, fourth edition. In Chapter 6, titled "Recognizing Homelessness," a drama structure is presented using an excerpt from the novel *Mr. Stink* by David Walliams.

In small groups or as a whole class, students can discuss the following:

- What do we know learn about Georgina and her family circumstances from the opening page of the novel?
- What words would you use to describe Georgina? Give reasons for your choices.
- How is Mama handling her tough situation?
- What do you wonder about when you read this passage?
- What are some challenges that Georgina, her brother, and her mother face by living in a car?
- Why is it important to keep the family circumstances a secret? Why might Georgina's best friend not keep this a secret?
- Predict what you think will happen to Georgina and her family.

Interviewing a Novel Character

1. Students work with a classmate to prepare a list of questions they would ask Georgina about her situation. Questions can be about her past life, her present life in a van, and her future life.
2. Students work in pairs to conduct an interview between Georgina and a reporter who is preparing an article on children who live in poverty. One student can assume the role of Georgina while the other student can be someone from a newspaper, a magazine, or a television show. The questions just prepared can be used to guide the interview.
3. Students switch roles. Those who are now reporters will be given the opportunity to interview other characters connected to Georgina, such as her mother, her father, her brother, her best friend, and her teacher.

How to Steal a Dog: Excerpt

After her father leaves the family virtually penniless, Georgina, her brother and her mother are forced to live in the family car. Even though her overworked mother demands that her children be patient, Georgina longs for change and is desperate to do anything that will improve the family situation — even if it means stealing a dog.

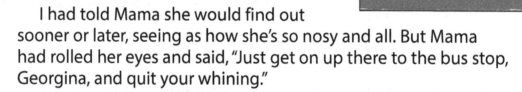

The day I decided to steal a dog was the same day my best friend, Luanne Godfrey, found out I lived in a car.

I had told Mama she would find out sooner or later, seeing as how she's so nosy and all. But Mama had rolled her eyes and said, "Just get on up there to the bus stop, Georgina, and quit your whining."

So that's what I did. I stood up there at the bus stop pretending like I still lived in Apartment 3B. I pretended like I didn't have mustard on my shirt from the day before. I pretended like I hadn't washed my hair in the bathroom of the Texaco gas station that very morning. And I pretended like my daddy hadn't just waltzed off and left us with nothing but three rolls of quarters and a mayonnaise jar full of wadded up dollar bills.

I guess I'm pretty good at pretending.

My brother, Toby, however, is not so good at pretending. When Mama told him to get on up to the bus stop and quit his whining, he cried and carried on like the baby he is.

Printed with permission from Square Fish Publishers.

Pembroke Publishers © 2020 *Teaching Tough Topics* by Larry Swartz   ISBN 978-1-55138-341-5

Discussion — Living in Poverty

As a class, students can discuss information that they learned about Georgina and her family. A key focus for the discussion is the topic of living in poverty. Suggested questions:

- What did students learn about people who live in poverty from the in-role interview?
- How could a parent or a child be optimistic about the future?
- How might circumstances change?

Writing in Role — A Media Report on Poverty

Using information gathered from the in-role interview, reporters prepare an article or report to describe the plight of families forced to live in a car. The report could answer the following questions:

- Why would a person or a family be forced to live in a car or van?
- What are some specific challenges this person or family might face?
- Why do these families want or need to keep this situation a secret?
- What word(s) could be used to describe someone in these circumstances?
- What possibilities await Georgina and her family?

Great Books for a Tough Topic

Picture Books

Avingaq, Susan, and Maren Vsetula (illus Charlene Chua). *The Pencil*

Boelts, Maribeth (illus. Noah Z. Jones). *Those Shoes*

Bunting, Eve (illus. Ronald Himler). *Fly Away Home*

—— (illus. Lauren Castillo). *Yard Sale*

Cooper, Melrose. *Gettin' Through Thursday*

De la Peña, Matt (illus. Christian Robinson). *Last Stop on Market Street*

Garay, Luis. *The Kite*

Gunning, Monica (illus. Elaine Pedlar). *A Shelter in Our Car*

Hathorn, Libby. *Way Home*

Hood, Susan (illus. Sally Wern Comport). *Ada's Violin: The Story of the Recycled Orchestra of Paraguay*

Mills, Lauren. *The Rag Coat*

Milway, Katie Smith (illus. Eugenie Fernandes). *One Hen: How One Small Loan Made a Big Difference*

—— (illus. Eugenie Fernandes). *Mimi's Village: And How Basic Health Care Transformed It*

McCarney, Rosemary A. (illus. Yvonne Cathcart). *Being Me*

McGovern, Ann (illus. Marni Backer). *The Lady in the Box*

McPhail, David M. *The Teddy Bear*

Rosen, Michael (illus. Becca Stadtlander). *The Greatest Table*

Smothers, Ethel Footman (illus. John Holyfield). *The Hard-Times Jar*

Spilsbury, Louise A. (illus. Hanane Kai). *Poverty and Hunger* (nonfiction)

Sturgis, Brenda Reeves (illus. Jo-Shin Lee). *Still a Family*

Walters, Eric (illus. Eugenie Fernandes). *Hope Springs*

Wild, Margaret (illus. Anne Spudvilas). *Woolvs in the Sitee*
Williams, Laura E. (illus. Craig Orback). *The Can Man*
Williams, Vera B. *A Chair for My Mother*
Woodson, Jacqueline. *Each Kindness*
Wyeth, Sharon Dennis (illus. Chris K. Soentpiet). *Something Beautiful*

Novels

Applegate, Katherine. *Crenshaw*
Auxier, Jonathan. *Sweep: The Story of a Girl and Her Monster*
Braden, Ann. *The Benefits of Being an Octopus*
Burg, Ann E. *Serafina's Promise: A Novel in Verse*
D'Adamo, Francesco (trans. Ann Leonori). *Iqbal: A Novel*
Estes, Eleanor (illus. Louis Slobodkin). *The Hundred Dresses*
Helget, Nicole. *The End of the Wild*
Kadarusman, Michelle. *Girl of the Southern Sea*
Levitin, Sonia (illus. Guy Porfirio). *Junk Man's Daughter*
Little, Jean. *Willow and Twig*
Nielsen, Susin. *No Fixed Address* (Also: *Word Nerd*)
O'Connor, Barbara. *How to Steal a Dog*
Pinkney, Andrea Davis (illus. Shane W. Evans). *The Red Pencil*
Ryan, Pam Muñoz. *Esperanza Rising*
Sher, Emil. *Young Man with Camera*
Spinelli, Jerry. *Maniac Magee*
Venkatraman, Padma. *The Bridge Home*
Voight, Cynthia. Homecoming (trilogy)
Walliams, David. *Mr. Stink*

Young Adult

Booth, Coe. *Tyrell*
Holman, Felice. *Slake's Limbo: 121 Days*
Myers, Walter Dean. *Scorpions*
Ogle, Rex. *Free Lunch* (autobiography)
Paterson, Katherine. *Lyddie*
Paulsen, Gary. *The Crossing*
Rowell, Rainbow. *Eleanor & Park*
Thomas, Angie. *On the Come Up*
Walters, Eric. *Shattered*

The Global Read Aloud: 2019

In *The Bridge Home* by Padma Venkatraman, two sisters run away from home and learn that life on the streets in Chennai, India, is brutal. When the girls meet up with two boys, they find shelter on an abandoned bridge and come to rely on one another through hunger, fear, and the fight for freedom.

This book was chosen as the Global Read Aloud title for 2019. The Global Read Aloud (GRA) is a program where teachers, librarians, and bookstores choose one book to read aloud during a set six-week period. The goal is to make as many global connections as possible.

Chapter 7

Death, Loss, and Remembrance

"Grief does not change you, Hazel. It reveals you."
— From *The Fault in Our Stars* by John Green

After the last shovel of dirt was patted in place, I sat down and let my mind drift back through the years.
— From *Where the Red Fern Grows* by Wilson Rawls

The crickets felt it was their duty to warn everybody that summertime cannot last forever. Even on the most beautiful days in the whole year — the days when summer is changing into autumn — the crickets spread the rumour of sadness and change.
— From *Charlotte's Web* by E. B. White

This chapter is dedicated to my nephew Solomon (1980–2014).

I often ask teachers to recall novels from their school days that they remember and without a doubt the classic title *Charlotte's Web* by E. B. White, written in 1952, comes to the top of the list. How many adults remember a teacher reading this book aloud in class? And how many remember the teacher (and perhaps the students around the teacher) shedding a tear or sobbing? One teacher I met recently commented, "It's hard for me to read this book to a group of students 'cause I know I'll cry." My answer: "Go ahead and cry!" Let the students know that books can touch you deeply and let them know how they do so by perhaps sharing insights or connections to the story. In this way you are showing them that you are doing what good readers do, and that you are human. The story about barnyard friends, a talking spider, and a pig about to be slaughtered is mostly offered as a read-aloud in Grade 2 or 3 classrooms. Few adults remember reading this book independently (it is a book worth rereading as a grown-up).

Preparing or Protecting Children: The Conundrum

From *Censorship Goes to School*

"Together we [teachers and parents] must forge a curriculum that will allow children freedom to read, freedom to think, and freedom to challenge and make their own decisions as lifelong learners."

— David Booth (1992, 13)

Yet *Charlotte's Web* continues to be banned in some communities, its talking animals criticized as blasphemous and unnatural and its story of a dying spider judged as inappropriate subject matter for a children's book. *Bridge to Terabithia* is another book that frequently appears on censored lists of children's books. I was fortunate to hear the author, Katherine Paterson, speak on the topic of censorship and remember listening to her claim that it is important for us to "prepare, not protect" our students from what may seem to be sensitive issues. In the interview on pages 107 and 108, Paterson shares her wise views about death in children's literature.

Books Can Foster Understanding of Death and Loss

When parents are faced with the sad news of a death in the family, they often have a genuine concern to find a book that may help their young children understand dying and loss.

Many picture books provide fictional narratives that will help children begin to understand the grieving process. Quite a few of these books centre on animals (e.g., *The Tenth Good Thing About Barney* by Judith Viorst, *Badger's Parting Gifts* by Susan Varley, *The Dead Bird* by Margaret Wise Brown, and *The Day Tiger Rose Said Goodbye* by Jane Yolen).

Novels where a dog has died have been responsible for many saddened hearts and shed tears (e.g., *Stone Fox* by John Reynolds Gardiner and *Where the Red Fern Grows* by Wilson Rawls). As students develop as readers, they will likely encounter events in fantasy and realistic fiction where a person has died (e.g., *A Taste of Blackberries* by Doris Buchanan Smith, *A Monster Calls* by Patrick Ness, and *The Fault in Our Stars* by John Green). Such books offer insight into human loss.

Presenting a book that helps students deal with a death in their life may answer questions, raise questions, and console them. Still, as much as any book can accomplish, having private conversations with others, where personal stories and feelings are exchanged, can help strengthen students coping with loss.

Death Affects Everyone

What is a more equitable topic than that of living and dying? Everyone dies. Understanding customs and practices observed in different religions provides a forum for considering diversity.

Death, it seems, is everywhere. Children will likely be faced with dying characters in the television shows and animated films they watch. If watching or reading the news, they will also encounter stories of murder, killing, and death almost every day. These events, as well as close personal encounters with death, can disturb students. The topic of death, loss, and remembrance is included in this book because it is recognized as a tough topic for teachers to help young people address.

Up-Close Encounters with Death

In my 25 years of teaching, death has edged its way into the classroom community. For several years, we had hamsters as a class pet and if you visit the garden in front of the public school, you might find a hamster cemetery that commemorates Mikey, Nike, Cappuccino, and Fluffy. One day, a punch in the heart came when we learned that one of the students in my Grade 4 class had died of leukemia. We talked about Andrew, told stories of Andrew's kindnesses, and celebrated his life in writing. The death of my father, the passing of our beloved school librarian, Ms. Checkeris, Amanda's hurt when she had to put down her pet cat, the death of a student's grandparent . . . these were tough topic events that filtered into my program over the years. Dealing with a personal story of death that a student encounters cannot be preplanned, but it is important that educators be sensitive and help students become sensitive, as well, as a vehicle for equity, diversity, and empathy.

Students of all ages will encounter a story of the death of a pet or of someone in their family, their school community, or their neighborhood. Knowing someone who has died because of old age, of an illness, of an accident, of a killing, or of suicide is the tough stuff of life. Never easy to handle.

In our classrooms we can choose to introduce book titles as a community, small-group, or independent experience. If we as teachers are aware of a loss or tragedy in a student's life, we might shy away from first introducing the topic through literature. We might talk with a grieving student privately. When we share books or introduce activities to the classroom, we never know what may trigger a student's story or memory. In a holistic curriculum of worth, for which we must strive, there must be a place to promote affective learning — learning that recognizes our students' feelings and emotions. Our work in dealing with a tough topic such as death — work that reaches and touches readers' hearts — can help lead to coping and comfort.

The Perspective feature that follows explores further the conundrum of whether to shield children from the theme of death or prepare them for possible encounters with its reality through children's literature.

PERSPECTIVE

Dealing with Bereavement Through Children's Literature: An Interview with Katherine Paterson

by Joyce Marcel

This feature is an excerpt from an article by Joyce Marcel, published in *Vermont Business Magazine* (June 2017). It is reprinted by permission of the author with thanks.

Bridge to Terabithia ranks eighth on the American Library Association's list of most commonly challenged books in the United States. That means her books inspire attempts at censorship. It's a good list to be on: Stephen King, Mark Twain, Toni Morrison, Judy Blume, Kurt Vonnegut and Jack London, among others, are also on it. What about a children's book can attract such censorship? Death, that's what. For example, one of the two main characters in *Bridge to Terabithia* dies unexpectedly and to the reader, it is quite a shock.

"How could you kill off Leslie?" was practically the first thing out of my mouth after we sat down to talk. For those who haven't read the book — and since it was published in 1977 and later filmed twice, I don't think I need a spoiler alert — it tells the story of two rural youngsters, a boy named Jesse and a girl named Leslie, both outsiders at school, who become great friends and create an imaginary and magical world called Terabithia in the forest; it's on the other side of a small stream that they cross by swinging on a rope, one at a time.

Then, when Jesse is off on a day trip with his teacher, he comes back to learn that the stream has swollen, the rope has broken, and Leslie has fallen and died. Her death leaves the reader unprepared and devastated, just as it leaves Jesse.

It was Paterson's decision to have one of her main characters die — instead of breaking an arm or leg, for example — that has garnered her the most criticism.

"I get these letters from adults saying death is not an appropriate topic for 10-year-olds," Paterson said. "But I had two children who lost friends. David was eight and Mary was four when friends died. It's not appropriate but it happens."

One problem with "*Terabithia*" and death is that it might be read to children who are too young — or like myself, too old — to deal with it.

"Teachers who love the book decide to use it with kids who are too young for it," Paterson said. "There's a difference between intellectual age and emotional age. Third graders are too young for the book. Fourth graders? Some are OK and some are not. I worry about children who still need a fairy tale. Is there a dividing line between children who need a fairy tale and children who need a book that reflects their life? It differs from child to child. And it's a book I really hope parents will read with their children. It gives you a safe place to talk about hard topics. I understand it's more profitable for me to have the book read in classrooms, because they buy all these copies. But my preference is for a child sitting close to a parent."

Children's books which feature death run counter to an American squeamishness about the subject.

"Death, a terrible thing for a child," Paterson said. "Loss is hard. Now people say, 'I gave the book to this child because they've had this terrible loss.' But it should be a reversal. They should read it before anyone dies. I get a lot of young adults who write to me. One I remember most clearly is a young man in college. He was home for vacation at Christmas time and he found out his best friend had been killed in an automobile accident on the way home for vacation. He went to his childhood room and found *Bridge to Terabithia* and it was such a comfort to him. If he hadn't had it when he was 10 or 11, he wouldn't have had it when he was 19."

This kind of feedback jibes with the Laura Ingalls Wilder folks, who wrote that Paterson's "unflinching yet redemptive treatment of tragedy and loss helped pave the way for ever more realistic writing for young people."

The character of Leslie is based on a real child, a close friend of Paterson's second son, David. In her 2014 memoir, *Stories of My Life*, she relates what happened:

"While the family was on vacation at Bethany Beach, on a day when the lifeguards sensed no danger from thunder far off in the distance, a joyful little girl, dancing on a rock above the crowded beach, was felled by a bolt of lightning from the sky. How was I to make sense of this tragedy for my child? I couldn't make sense of it for myself, so eventually, I began to write a story, because I knew that a story has to make sense."

So that's how you dared to kill off Leslie, I said.

"Well, you know," Paterson said, "it had to be done. But I do apologize. It was one of the hardest things I ever did, and to do it I had to stop writing for a while just to keep her alive."

The Language and Vocabulary of Death and Loss

Begin by establishing these key words with students:

- **Death** can be defined as the action or fact of dying or of being killed: the end of the life of a person or organism.
- **Loss**, in this context, is related to grief over losing someone in your life. The death of someone who has been close to you is considered a loss because that person has been taken away from you.
- **Remembrance** is a memory or recollection of someone or something. It is the action of remembering the dead, especially in a ceremony or special service.

You may also want to explore other words and phrases for conveying that someone has died. Synonyms for *death* include these: demise, dying, end, passing, passing away, passing on, loss of life, expiration, departure from life, final exit, eternal rest. Avoiding idioms such as "kick the bucket" is a good idea.

Recognizing Diversity in Death

- Invite students who speak language(s) other than English to suggest words meaning death in those other languages. Responses could be listed on the board, for example, *dood* (Dutch), *tod* (German), *morte* (Italian), and *tur vong* (Vietnamese).
- Provide students with an opportunity to explore words that they may or may not be familiar with. Hand out copies of the line master "The ABCs of Death: Key Vocabulary" (see page 110). The wide range of sometimes rather obscure words represents diversity in the experience of death. After students read the list, they can identify familiar words by placing a check mark in the designated spot. They can designate unfamiliar words with a question mark. Students then meet with others to share definitions of known terms. Finally, they can use dictionaries to discover and record the meanings of three to five unfamiliar vocabulary words.

Working with a line master like "The ABCs of Death: Key Vocabulary" can nudge a student to share thoughts about the recent loss of a relative, something that you may or may not be aware of.

Opening Up the Topic of Death

This activity invites students to make text-to-self connections, in this case, to a poem about death by Langston Hughes. To demonstrate how to make connections to the text, teachers can share a personal story that the words of Langston Hughes remind them of.

> I loved my friend
> He went away from me
> There's nothing more to say
> The poem ends
> Soft as it began —
> I loved my friend.

1. Share aloud the poem by Langston Hughes. Invite students to share stories that may come to mind about being sad because someone "went away."
   - Tell a story about a time you had to say good-bye to a friend or relative who moved away.
   - Describe a time (or tell a story) about a friend, relatively, community member, or pet who "went away" from you because of death.
2. Invite students to "turn and talk" with one or two others and tell personal stories about death and loss. Encourage students to share stories that come to mind as others tell their own stories. For example, when Stacey tells a story about her hamster dying, Aaron might tell a story about going to a veterinarian to have his cat put down. When William tells a story about his grandmother in hospital, Rebecca might tell a story about visiting her grandfather in the nursing home because he was in palliative care.

Model Lesson 1: Eliciting Oral Narratives Through Literature

This lesson works well for students in all grades.

Featured Text: Always with You *by Eric Walters, illustrated by Carloe Liu*

Picture books where a person or animal dies can help students understand death and loss; remember stories about family members and friends they have lost; and perhaps provide insights into dealing with grief. In his picture book *Always with You*, Eric Walters takes readers on a journey through the pivotal moments in

The ABCs of Death: Key Vocabulary

- Place a check mark (√) beside all the vocabulary words related to death that you are familiar with.
- Place a question mark (?) beside five vocabulary words related to death that you are NOT familiar with.
- Place an asterisk (*) beside three to five vocabulary words that you would most like to know the definition of.

Work in groups of three or four to discuss the vocabulary words below. What definitions and explanations would you suggest for words that you are familiar with?

____ afterlife
____ autopsy
____ bereavement
____ brain death
____ burial
____ catacomb
____ corpse
____ cremation
____ crypt
____ death
____ decomposition
____ embalming
____ epitaph
____ eulogy
____ euthanasia
____ feeding tube
____ grief
____ Hades
____ hearse
____ hospice
____ immortality
____ karma
____ life support
____ living will

____ livor mortis
____ mausoleum
____ mourning
____ nirvana
____ obituary
____ palliative care
____ pyre
____ Qingming
____ reincarnation
____ ritual
____ sarcophagus
____ shroud
____ sky burial
____ soul
____ thanatology
____ tomb
____ undertaker
____ underworld
____ vigil
____ wake
____ widow
____ will
____ zombie

Investigating Definitions

- Use a dictionary or the Internet to find definitions for the words (three to five of them) whose meanings you want to know.
- Collaborate with your classmates to prepare a Glossary of Terms connected to the topic of death. You will be assigned a single word from the list to investigate and determine the meaning of. Definitions can be gathered into a resource and accompanied by drawings.

Pembroke Publishers © 2020 *Teaching Tough Topics* by Larry Swartz   ISBN 978-1-55138-341-5

Emily's life, for example, her first day of school, graduation day, and her wedding. For each of these events, Emily receives grandfatherly advice from an important person in her life who has died: her grandfather. Messages from him appear as fold-out letters throughout the book. This story is about dealing with grief, experiencing life stages, and remembering those who will always be with us.

The Stories of Our Lives

The best response to a story, such as a picture book, is to tell another story.

The stories of our lives are just waiting to be told. Sometimes a book, movie, play, or news report reminds us of our own experiences. Often, when other people tell stories of their lives, the stories of our own lives are awakened. If we feel comfortable with people, we will reveal stories that have been tucked away in our minds. These stories can pop out of our mouths, released by the human need to share them. Teachers and their students have a wealth of stories waiting to be elicited and shared.

Reading is a bring-and-take experience. When we introduce children's literature to students, we can be explicit and invite responses to a book title or theme. We can ask: "What stories from your own life or the life of someone you know come to mind when you read [hear] this title?" By doing so we are encouraging students to give meaning to their stories. When students tell personal stories, they are not only choosing to talk about their life experiences, but also building a dimension of who they are. We are also building a story forum in the classroom where students connect to literature through shared personal narratives while deepening connections to one another.

When we present a piece of children's literature to our students, it can also elicit natural responses. Some picture books, such as *Always with You*, explicitly deal with the loss of a person or a pet and can inspire students to share stories from their own lives. When a character, animal, or human dies in the story, it may make readers pause and think about stories of death. Some students may choose to share them in discussion or writing.

Inspiring Oral Narratives

First, here is a general outline based on the read-aloud of a story from children's literature to the class.

- Before the story, activate students' prior experiences. For example, if you plan to read *The Dead Bird* by Margaret Wise Brown, you could ask students whether they have seen any animal deaths in their community.
- During the story, encourage spontaneous responses — teachers cannot plan for what will trigger a memory. Do a think-aloud while reading to demonstrate how the story has prompted a text-to-self connection.
- After the story, ask: "Was there anything in the story that reminded you of something from your own life or someone you know? Did the story remind you of other books or poems you have read, or of YouTube videos, movies, or theatre plays you have seen?" Students can share stories from their lives or reading in small groups and then with the whole class (or vice versa).

A Classroom Demonstration

My visit to Elaine Eisen's Grade 4 classroom provided an opportunity for students to share personal stories about the topic of death. Before reading the picture book *Always with You*, I shared my own stories, telling the students about my nephew Solomon, who died of cancer at 33 years of age, and about the death of a special colleague, Brian, whom I often think about when sharing a good book with young people. The stories that I told seemed to inspire some students to share their own stories about pets, relatives, and acquaintances who had passed.

I read the picture book aloud to the students without interruption. I encouraged the students to be aware of what was happening in their heads as they listened to the story. I knew that they were very familiar with the comprehension strategy of text-to-self connections. I advised them that stories would likely pop up unexpectedly as they listened to Walters's narrative.

The community of readers revealed their stories: first, as a turn-and-talk to discover what those around them were thinking, and subsequently, as a class sharing.

For a final activity, students were instructed to write a story, inspired by the picture book and the personal out-loud stories they might have chosen to share. Here are a few of the stories that the students composed.

> "This story reminds me of my grandmother, Farideh, who died at the age of 64 of cancer. Even though my grandmother is not in this world, her spirit lives on in another. She will always be with me. I know it." LM

> "One of my grandma's sisters died from cancer. Just now as I write this, I wonder if she's watching over my grandma, her sisters, and, of course, all the families. I've never actually met her which makes me sort of upset, but I still think she's watching me." FG

> "There was once a bird that always used to fly around my house. I would always leave it food, but one day I looked out the window. The bird died. I made it a grave. The sad thing is, right before her death, the bird gave birth to two other birds. I fed them and helped them until they were able to fly. They still fly around my house. I named them Salt and Pepper." RP

> "This book reminds me of my Grandfather, who is always with me. When he died in October, I felt bad. He had a heart attack. I know my grandfather is in heaven. I hope he is reading his science fiction novels up there. And having bubble baths. And eating fresh food." JT

When students tell stories orally, they are rehearsing a way to share their thoughts in writing. In many cases, it is important for students to write a personal narrative they have told in order to give the anecdote significance. In this way, the event is a meaningful way to integrate reading (the book), speaking (oral narrative), and writing (memoir).

Model Lesson 2: Researching Diverse Ways of Honoring Death

This lesson is most suitable for students in Grades 6 to 9.

Selected Text: After Life: Ways We Think About Death *by Merrie-Ellen Wilcox*

After Life: Ways We Think About Death by Merrie-Ellen Wilcox helps students to think further about the topic of death and to understand what it means to be human. The nonfiction resource presents a clear, informative look at the questions that students might have about dying, the myths from different cultures, and the ways people around the world honor loved ones who have passed.

Part A: Sharing Family Experiences of Death

By sharing stories about how death is honored in their families, older students can make comparisons between death in different cultures and religions. They can draw on what they know about how death is marked in their culture by considering questions like these:

- What are some important burial practices?
- What practices usually happen at a place of worship? at home?
- Is there a period of mourning? How long is it?
- How might clothing, foods, and prayer be a part of the mourning period?

Part B: Researching and Reporting Facts About Death

Students can work independently or in pairs to research and report information related to death. They can use the Internet for some of their research. Some suggested inquiry topics are these:

the afterlife	mummification
cremation	death in different cultures
the Black Death	the eight stages of grief
coffins	what happens to a body after death

Great Books for a Tough Topic

Picture Books

Brown, Margaret Wise (illus. Christian Robinson). *The Dead Bird*
Burningham, John. *Granpa*
Jeffers, Oliver. *The Heart and the Bottle*
Levis, Caron (illus. Charles Santoso). *Ida, Always*
Lunde, Stein Erik (illus. Oyvind Torseter). *My Father's Arms Are a Boat*
Oskarsson, Bardur. *The Flat Rabbit*
Ringtved, Glenn (illus. Charlotte Pardi). *Cry, Heart, But Never Break*
Rosen, Michael (illus. Quentin Blake). *Michael Rosen's Sad Book*
Varley, Susan. *Badger's Parting Gifts*
Viorst, Judith (illus. Erik Blegvad). *The Tenth Good Thing About Barney*
Walters, Eric (illus. Carloe Liu). *Always with You*
Yolen, Jane (Jim LaMarche). *The Day Tiger Rose Said Goodbye*

Novels

Anderson, John David. *Finding Orion*
Appelt, Kathi, and Alison McGhee. *Maybe a Fox*
Benjamin, Ali. *The Thing About Jellyfish*
MacLachlan, Patricia. *Edward's Eyes*
———. *My Father's Words*
Ness, Patrick (illus. Jim Kay). *A Monster Calls*
Paterson, Katherine. *Bridge to Terabithia*

Pennypacker, Sara (illus. Jon Klassen). *Pax*
Rylant, Cynthia. *Missing May*
Smith, Doris Buchanan. *A Taste of Blackberries*
White, E. B. *Charlotte's Web*

Young Adult

Asher, Jay. *Thirteen Reasons Why*
Francis, Brian. *Break in Case of Emergency*
Green, John. *The Fault in Our Stars*
Jocelyn, Marthe. *Would You*
Nelson, Jandy. *I'll Give You the Sun*
Niven, Jennifer. *All the Bright Places*
Sloan, Holly Goldberg. *Counting by 7s*
Zusak, Markus. *The Book Thief*

Other

Fitch, Sheree. *You Won't Always Be This Sad: A Book of Moments* (poetry)
Thornhill, Jan. *I Found a Dead Bird* (nonfiction)
Wilcox, Merrie-Ellen. *After Life: Ways We Think About Death* (nonfiction)

Chapter 8

Gender Identity and Homophobia

"Boys don't wear dresses," Becky snipped.
Morris smiled as he swished, crinkled and clicked back to his spaceship.
"This boy does!"

— From *Morris Micklewhite and the Tangerine Dress* by Christine Baldacchino, illustrated by Isabelle Malenfant

"It's just . . ." George sighed. "I just thought that . . . you know . . . if I were Charlotte in the play, my mom might . . ."
"See that you're a girl?"
"Yeah," said George. It felt funny to hear Kelly call her a girl — but in a good way, like a tickling in her stomach that reminded her she was real.

— From *George* by Alex Gino

A fear of small spaces is known as *claustrophobia*. A fear of spiders is known as *arachnophobia*. A fear of homosexuals is known as *homophobia*. What are the roots of these fears? How can these fears be conquered? Can they be conquered?

Considering a Spectrum of Equity

Any program that teaches about equity needs to find a place for confronting and exploring the tough topic of homophobia and gender identity. There are many reasons why someone develops a phobia, but when it comes to a fear of others, some people are afraid of what they don't know, and some are simply taught to hate or distrust what they don't know or understand. In schools, students are very much influenced by their peers, and it's tempting to hate others who are not "part of the crowd."

Even at a very young age, children know that they are different because they know whether they are a boy or a girl. They are also usually surrounded by a culture of pink and blue with the clothes they wear, the toys they play with, the hobbies and sports they participate in. As children grow older, however, they may come to question their sexual identity. The questions that many young people have are often kept hidden until they mature.

Students may come to accept and be curious about changing gender roles. Today many children live in same-sex marriage households, young children choose to wear clothes that may not be associated with their gender, and people, young and old, are discovering that they are genderfluid, questioning the sex that they were born with. In the United States, there are thought to be about 150 000 transgender teenagers. There may be only a small percentage of our student population who identify as transgender or genderfluid, but greater public awareness of the issue encourages more students to "come out" and transition. Bringing attention to these issues in the classroom is an important step in supporting awareness and acceptance of LGBTQ identity. Perhaps there is a place for discussions about this tough topic to emerge when addressing expectations in the Physical Education and Health curriculum.

Exploring Questions of Identity

Particularly in the past decade, there have been published many picture books and novels that help some readers identify with the fictional characters and answer questions about their own identities. To promote social justice, diversity, and equity, teachers need to consider including titles that address issues of gender and sexual identity. When teachers share literature that addresses this aspect of our identities, they are choosing to acknowledge, celebrate, and consider a significant aspect of the equity and diversity spectrum.

In my early years of teaching, I had only two picture books to turn to in order to address different gender behaviors: *William's Doll* by Charlotte Zolotow (1972) and *Oliver Button Is a Sissy* by Tomie dePaola (1979). Today, many novels introduce a sphere of queer characters that students can identify with or learn from. Today, we have Julián (*Julián Is a Mermaid*), Casey (*Sparkle Boy*), and *Jazz* (*I Am Jazz*) as picture book heroes to bring the topic into classrooms with young children.

The Teacher, the Girl, the Boy in a Dress

I have shared the picture book *Morris Micklewhite and the Tangerine Dress* by Christine Baldacchino with hundreds of children from Kindergarten to high school and with more than 1000 teachers in workshop presentations. Morris is a young boy who loves to wear a tangerine dress because it reminds him of the sun, tigers, and the color of his mother's hair. Morris is continually teased by his classmates because of his preferred choice of dress-up play. Morris bravely soldiers on until the taunting disturbs him; he then stays home from school to be comforted by his mother.

When Morris returns to school, a classmate, Becky, demands to wear the dress and snips, "Boys don't wear dresses!" This storybook character seems to represent those who have no problem teasing and taunting others because they are different or choose to behave differently. Does Becky understand why the dress is so important to Morris? What did Becky learn from her family? from society? Why is Becky so afraid of Morris's behavior? What will change Becky's thinking?

The book never fails to summon responses from listeners. These comments come from nine-year-old students:

"I feel sorry for Morris because nobody can tell you what to do."

"I don't know why the kids were so mean to Morris. They probably don't know why the dress was so important to him."

"I am afraid of what might happen to Morris when he gets older."

"Where was the teacher in the story? Maybe she was just watching Morris to see if he could solve problems on his own."

We can only infer that Morris's teacher was aware of what was going on in the classroom. We can infer that she had thoughtful conversations with Morris about his world of play and whether he pretends to hear others or not. We can predict (and hope for) positive conversations she might have with her young class to help them understand Morris's behavior. We hope that, as a caring compassionate teacher, she finds a place to educate the children in her classroom and conquer the attitudes and fears of those who are bothered by those who are different in their gender identity and those who are homosexual.

Ken Setterington is a children's book reviewer, a former librarian with the Toronto Public Library, which named him the first Children and Youth Advocate for Library Services, and an author. His books include *Mom and Mum Are Getting Married* and *Branded by the Pink Triangle*.

PERSPECTIVE

Children's Books: Making the World Understandable

by Ken Setterington

Children's books, whether board books and picture books for the young, simple read-aloud books for early readers, or novels and graphic novels for middle-grade readers, can introduce new ideas to children and expand their horizons. Recent publications in all these formats include titles that promote understanding of gender identity and can combat homophobia. Of course, they fulfill that task only when they are introduced to children. It is crucial to read them to children who may see themselves reflected in the books and to children who may not yet have encountered these issues but are curious.

Books help children understand how others are feeling. Empathy is developed through reading. A book about a boy who wants to wear a tangerine dress helps not only a little boy who wants to wear a dress, but other people who need to understand his interest in doing do. Normalizing families with same-sex parents helps children at a young age to see that families are built in a variety of ways. The earlier children learn about different family structures, the more accepting they become.

Recent books dealing with gender identity will help girls and boys who are questioning their own identities navigate their journeys. The books will be extremely useful for them, but the books may be even more useful as they introduce the concept to children who have never even thought about the topic.

Fostering empathy and respect for others while engaging readers in stories helps build a more inclusive world and reduces bullying. The unknown is always frightening, but children's books can help make the world more understandable.

PERSPECTIVE

Why Teach Students About Gender Identity and Homophobia

by Tara Goldstein and benjamin lee hicks

Homophobia is the fear, hatred, or intolerance of people who are homosexual and/or who express themselves in ways that challenge traditional gender roles. Homophobia may stem from a fear of associating with gay and lesbian people and/or of being perceived as gay or lesbian. Homophobic behaviors can range from (and beyond) telling jokes about lesbian, gay, or queer people to physical violence against people thought to be lesbian, gay, or queer (hicks 2019).

Address Gender-Based and Homophobic Bullying

It is important for teachers to talk about homophobia, as well as gender roles and identities, in their classrooms and schools because a large survey study of the experiences of LGBTQ students in Canadian schools, for example, tells us that 70 percent of the students who participated in the study, LGBTQ and non-LGBTQ, reported hearing expressions such as "that's so gay" every day at school and almost half (48%) reported hearing remarks such as "faggot," "lezbo," and "dyke" every day at school. More than one in five LGBTQ students (21%) reported being physically harassed or assaulted about their perceived sexual orientation or gender identity (Taylor and Peter 2011).

Tara's research on the experiences of LGBTQ families in Ontario schools, written up as a book of letters to teachers who want to learn how to work with issues of gender and sexuality in their classrooms, confirms the findings of the 2011 Canadian survey: incidents of gender-based and homophobic bullying are still prevalent in classrooms and schools and must be addressed by teachers, principals, and parents (Goldstein 2019). Although many people believe that gender-based and homophobic bullying is anti-social behavior, current research tells us pro-social behavior polices gender and sexuality in school (Goldstein 2019).

To stop bullying in a substantial and sustained way, schools need to create curriculum which teaches students that there are many ways to express their gender and sexuality and many ways to love. Teachers who bring LGBTQ-themed literature into their classroom tell us reading about LGBTQ lives can be a powerful way to talk about gender and sexuality with children and youth. A helpful website for finding contemporary books with lesbian, gay, bisexual, transgender, questioning, queer, gender-creative teen characters and themes is Lee Wind's *I'm Here, I'm Queer. What the Hell Do I Read?* (www.leewind.org). The website also includes a list of books with characters who are LGBTQ family members.

Three Key Concepts Clarified

When using children's literature to teach students about gender and sexuality, it is important for teachers to understand the differences between the terms *gender*, *sex*, and *sexual orientation*. Here are the definitions benjamin has written up in "The Unicorn Glossary," in Tara's 2019 book *Teaching Gender and Sexuality at School: Letters to Teachers*.

Gender: "Gender, or the lack thereof, is part of a person's identity" (Reiff Hill, Mays, and Mack 2013). It is an idea that originates in personal thought and feeling, but it is also important to consider the ways that even our own relationships *to* these ideas are socially constructed. Gender is personal. It is the way that you think and feel about yourself in relation to binary social definitions like "male" and "female" and your gender may also include a rejection of or variation on these ideas (hicks 2017). "Social ideas about gender stem from societal expectations of how a person should behave based on their sex" (Toronto District School Board [TDSB] 2014). "Societal expectations may vary by culture and consist of the attitudes, feelings, and behaviours that are associated with being female or male" (Bardwell 2012).

Sex: Includes physical (but still subjective) indicators like external genitalia, internal reproductive structures, chromosomes, hormone levels, and secondary sex characteristics such as breasts, facial and body hair, and patterns of body fat distribution. These characteristics are frequently assumed to be absolute and objective because medical models are fond of quantifying and sorting them into two discrete categories (male and female). In reality, sex is a continuum. The majority of people exist somewhere close to the areas of that continuum that we have called "male" and female," but there is also a vast middle space occupied by *intersex* persons (TDSB 2014).

Sexual Orientation: Refers to someone's desire in relation to intimate, emotional, and sexual relationships. This may be a lack of attraction to people of any gender (*asexual*), attraction in a binary system to people of the same gender (*homosexual, gay, lesbian*), people of the opposite gender (*heterosexual, straight*), people of either binary gender (*bisexual*), or people of any gender identity, including those that exist outside a binary system (*pansexual, polysexual, omnisexual, queer*). This attraction may remain static or may be fluid and change over time. When we talk about sexual orientation, we are largely discussing one's attraction to other people of certain gender identities and expressions; however, individuals may also hold preferences for certain physical bodies, including primary and secondary sexual characteristics. Others still are attracted primarily to the way another person's brain works (*sapiosexual*) (hicks 2017).

Parents' Advice to Teachers

Sometimes, teachers are reluctant to talk about gender and sexuality in their classrooms because they are worried about what their students' parents might think or say (Goldstein 2019, Letter 3). The parents who participated in Tara's 2014–20 research study on the experiences of LGBTQ families in Ontario elementary and secondary schools (www.lgbtqfamiliesspeakout.ca) remind teachers that at some time within their careers they will likely teach students who identify as LGBTQ and students whose parents or care takers identify as LGBTQ. These students, parents, and care takers have concerns about the hostile school culture that LGBTQ children and youth have to navigate. Teachers have the power and authority to create classroom and school cultures that expect and welcome LGBTQ students and families. As one parent, Syn Scully, told Tara in his interview, a teacher might be the only supportive adult a student has in their life: "And having that role is really powerful, you can do a lot of good . . . being the person that tries to pull in that help for those struggling ones is super important" (Goldstein and Scully 2018).

Tara Goldstein is an equity instructor at the Ontario Institute for Studies in Education, University of Toronto, as well as an author and a playwright. benjamin lee hicks is also at the Ontario Institute for Studies in Education, where he serves as a researcher.

References

Bardwell, S. 2012. *Gender and Sexuality: A Not-Necessarily-Comprehensive List of Terms.* Toronto: Unpublished paper, University of Toronto.

Goldstein, Tara. 2019. *Teaching Gender and Sexuality at School: Letters to Teachers.* New York: Taylor and Francis/Routledge. With contributions from benjamin lee hicks, Jenny Salisbury, and Pam Baer.

hicks, benjamin lee. 2017. "Gracefully Unexpected, Deeply Present and Positively Disruptive: Love and Queerness in Classroom Community." *Bank Street Occasional Paper Series* 2017 (37).

———. 2019. "The Unicorn Glossary." In *Teaching Gender and Sexuality at School: Letters to Teachers* by Tara Goldstein (New York: Taylor and Francis/Routledge).

Reiff Hill, Mel, Jay Mays, and Robin Mack. 2013. *The Gender Book.* Houston, TX: Marshall House Press.

Taylor, Catherine, and Tracey Peter. 2011. *Every Class in Every School: The First National Climate Survey on Homophobia, Biphobia, and Transphobia in Canadian Schools.* Final Report. Toronto: EGALE Canada Human Rights Trust.

Toronto District School Board. 2014. *Guidelines for the Accommodation of Transgender and Gender Independent/Non-Conforming Students and Staff.* Retrieved from http://www.tdsb.on.ca/AboutUs/Innovation/GenderBasedViolencePrevention/ AccommodationofTransgenderStudentsandStaff.aspx

The Language and Vocabulary of Gender Identity

LGBT is an adjective, an initialism that stands for lesbian, gay, bisexual, and transgender. The initialism is intended to emphasize the diversity of sexual and gender identities. The letter Q is often added to the initialism to represent queer or questioning (LGBTQ).

The Problem with Pronouns

It is often important to use language that implicitly or explicitly includes both men and women, making no distinction between the genders. Doing this can be tricky when it comes to pronouns. There are currently no personal pronouns in English that refer to someone (as opposed to something) without identifying whether the person is male or female.

Gender-neutral, gender-appropriate pronouns have a history of challenging our use of English, but in recent years they have been important to non-binary people who don't identify as either male or female. Using either *he* or *she* is inadequate, as is the term *he or she*, as it assumes binary gender.

Some people consider the use of *they* grammatically incorrect because it refers to more than one. Still, the use of *they* is becoming more widely accepted in both speech and writing. In everyday life, non-binary people usually state a preference for appropriate pronouns. For example, someone might say: "My name is Sasha. I use *they* and *them* pronouns."

Exploring Terms Related to Sexuality and Gender Identity

The line master on page 121 allows students to consider and understand definitions connected to the topic of sexuality and gender identity. Students match definitions (Column A) with key vocabulary terms (Column B). The line master also invites students to investigate definitions for other words. Students can then meet in groups to share definitions and discuss any confusions.

Opening Up the Topic of Homophobia

Homophobia is a fear of or negative bias against members of the LGBTQ community. Too often, students toss out the put-down "That's so gay!" Perhaps they do so to hurt others, or perhaps they speak without thinking. Perhaps the put-down comes from ignorance, perhaps from insecurity, perhaps from fear. By choosing to open up the topic of homophobia, teachers are helping students to understand what homophobia is, why some people are homophobic, and why being homophobic is against social justice, equity, and diversity beliefs.

A line master titled "Thinking About Homophobia" appears on pages 122 and 123. It provides a way for students to consider what they already know about homophobia and why some people are subject to this fear.

The Language of Sexuality and Gender Identity

Part A: Matching Definitions

Work independently to match the definitions in Column A with the words listed in words listed in the Word Pool; record the correct words in Column B. Then, work with a partner to compare answers and discuss definitions.

> **Example:** Gender identity that doesn't fit neatly into male/female categories.   ANDROGYNOUS

Column A	**Column B**
Identifies as a third gender that blends male and female characteristics.	_____
The opposite of transgender: gender matches their birth sex.	_____
Gender identity that doesn't fit neatly into male/female categories.	_____
Feels their gender is different than their birth sex.	_____
Physically attracted to both men and women.	_____
Physically attracted to people of the opposite gender.	_____
Physically attracted to people of the same gender.	_____
Not physically attracted to anyone.	_____
Fear or negative bias against LGBTQ community members.	_____
One who sees self as part of the LGBTQ community.	_____
Sometimes identifies as male and sometimes as female.	_____

> **Word Pool:** queer, lesbian, homosexual, CIS, bisexual, intersex, asexual, two-spirit, heterosexual, genderfluid, androgynous, homophobia, transgender, gender-queer, crossdresser, questioning

Part B: Discovering Definitions

There are more words listed than the number of definitions. Which words in the Word Pool were not chosen? Use a dictionary or the Internet to find definitions for three to five words that were not explained in Part A.

Pembroke Publishers © 2020 *Teaching Tough Topics* by Larry Swartz   ISBN 978-1-55138-341-5

Thinking About Homophobia

Part A: Understanding Homophobia
- Read the following list that outlines some reasons why people might be homophobic.
- Choose the **three** reasons you think are the most accurate. Put a star beside each of them.
- Work in groups of four to six to compare and assess reasons.

   Which reason identified was the most common?
   Which of the 10 reasons were not mentioned? Why do you think that is?
   Can you think of other possible reasons that are not on this list?

Why Do Some People Fear or Hate Others?
_____ 1. They are afraid of what they don't know.
_____ 2. They feel intimidated by others who are comfortable with their own identity.
_____ 3. They are taught to hate or distrust what they don't know or understand.
_____ 4. They absorb negative attitudes from family members, their social community, or the media.
_____ 5. Peer pressure — people go along with cruel things because they want to be accepted by others.
_____ 6. People are insecure: they take out their anxieties about themselves on others, especially members of minorities.
_____ 7. They are questioning their own sexual identity, perhaps being LGBTQ themselves.
_____ 8. They are comfortable about having power over others: of being bullies.
_____ 9. They hold on to what they think is normal and are unwilling to be tolerant of those who are different.
_____ 10. Religion tells them that homosexuality is wrong.

Answer the following:

What might you say to someone who is homophobic?

_____

_____

_____

How might ideas on the above list be applicable to people who seem to be racist?

_____

_____

_____

Pembroke Publishers © 2020 *Teaching Tough Topics* by Larry Swartz   ISBN 978-1-55138-341-5

Thinking About Homophobia *continued*

Part B: Facing Homophobic Behavior
Put yourself in the shoes of someone exposed to homophobic behavior.
- Read the list of actions a person might take to deal with someone who has tormented them or others.
- Choose **three** actions from the list that would best help confront someone who is mean to you. Put a star beside each of them..
- Work in groups of four or six to compare and discuss your choices. Consider these questions:

  Which approach is the most effective?
  What are the strengths and challenges of each of the actions you have identified?
  Which recommendations from the list of 10 actions were not noted? Why?

Actions to Consider Taking

_____ 1. Stand up for yourself.
_____ 2. Tell someone.
_____ 3. Stick with friends.
_____ 4. Make friends with the tormentor.
_____ 5. Ignore them.
_____ 6. Read literature or nonfiction reference material to understand how others deal with the situation.
_____ 7. Be an activist. For example, write a letter to the editor or join a Gay-Straight Alliance.
_____ 8. Seek out a role model who has successfully dealt with homophobia.
_____ 9. Find stories on the Internet (YouTube) that inspire you. Share with others.
_____ 10. Gather courage to write a letter or email to someone who has demonstrated hate to you or others.

Answer the following:

What advice might you give to someone who is being tormented by others because of their sexuality or gender identity?

_____

_____

Do you think the recommendations listed on this page could apply to someone who has been a victim of racism? Explain.

_____

_____

Pembroke Publishers © 2020 *Teaching Tough Topics* by Larry Swartz   ISBN 978-1-55138-341-5

Model Lesson 1: Responding to a Picture Book Through Prompts

Featured Text: See the text box "Picture Books That Explore Genderfluidity."

This lesson works especially well with younger students.

A number of picture books deal with genderfluidity. Fictional characters challenge gender stereotypes, helping readers to be tolerant and accepting of differences. The graphic organizer on page 126 invites students to share their thoughts about such a story by completing sentence stems: I learned, I felt, I wondered, and I remember. Space is provided for students to record "something I would say to the main character." Students can also make a prediction about the character by creating an illustration that shows them at some future date.

Genderfluidity is when gender identity shifts between masculine and feminine. A genderfluid person does not identify themselves as having a fixed gender.

For this activity any of the following recent picture book titles can be read aloud and used to promote a response. A further list of recommended titles is outlined in Great Books for a Tough Topic on page 129.

Picture Books That Explore Genderfluidity

The Boy & the Bindi by Vivek Shraya, illustrated by Rajini Perera
> The experiences of a young boy who is obsessed with wearing a Bindi just like his mother does.

Jack (Not Jackie) by Erica Silverman, illustrated by Holly Hatam
> How will Jackie's family accept her when she chooses to identify and experience life more as "Jack"?

Julián Is a Mermaid by Jessica Love
> A boy imagines he is a mermaid and is just fine being who he wants to be!

Morris Micklewhite and the Tangerine Dress by Christine Baldacchino, illustrated by Isabelle Malenfant
> During play time, Morris loves wearing a tangerine dress, even though he gets teased by his classmates.

Worm Loves Worm by J. J. Austrian, illustrated by Mike Curato
> Worm and Worm are getting married. Who will be the bride? Who will be the groom?

Model Lesson 2: Interpreting a Dialogue Script

Featured Text: Jake's Progress by Andrew Moodie

This lesson is recommended for older students (Grades 6 to 9).

A script is a text that demands to be read out loud and is therefore significant in helping students develop their interpretation skills. Working with script provides an opportunity to engage the students in an active, collaborative experience while providing a meaningful literacy event: one that integrates reading and oral communication, literacy, and drama.

A scripted scene can serve as a key piece of text for responding to the themes and issues inherent in the text. When students read aloud, they are digging deeper into the meaning behind the words and can experience incidents from different points of view. Readers become part of the dialogue — not just observers.

This script is one of nine short scripts by Canadian playwrights that appear in the resource *More Than a Play*, published by the Elementary Teachers' Federation of Ontario (ETFO). *Permission to reprint the excerpt has been granted by the Elementary Teachers' Federation of Ontario.*

As students bring the *Jake's Progress* excerpt to life, they experience the thoughts, feelings, and understandings of characters involved and work towards empathizing with the characters who are dealing with homophobia.

Introducing *Jake's Progress*: The Issue

The dialogue script excerpt on page 127 is the opening scene of the play *Jake's Progress* by Andrew Moodie. The genders of these roles are interchangeable. Characters, including Pat, could be male or female. This scene introduces two characters. One student has been given the responsibility of passing on homework to a classmate, Pat, who has been absent from school. Knowing that Pat has two fathers, this student is reluctant to visit the classmate's house.

Guide to Interpreting and Exploring the Scene

1. Students read the script independently.
2. The teacher reads the role of Terri; students in unison read the role of Jake.
3. The class repeats activity #2, switching roles.
4. Students work in pairs to read the script aloud. Partner A reads Terri's lines; partner B reads Jake's lines.
5. Pairs repeat activity #4, switching roles.
6. Discuss the script:
   - How would you describe each of the characters in this script?
   - What is the problem established in the opening scene? Why is this a problem?
   - What other characters might be introduced into this play? Why might the author include these characters?
   - What do you think will happen as the play unfolds? How will Jake make "progress"?
7. Each partner chooses a role to portray. Before reading the dialogue script, students consider what kind of attitude the students bring to the situation, for example, angry, frustrated, mellow, surprised, sad, or nervous. Pairs reread the script keeping the attitude or emotions in mind as they interpret the words.
8. Pairs repeat activity #7. Each partner reads the same part but finds a new attitude to help them say the lines. Some pairs may choose to have the same attitude.
9. Pairs discuss how they think this scene might be portrayed on stage. Would one or both characters be seated? What might the characters be doing? What gestures might they use? Students rehearse the scene as if getting ready to present it theatrically.
10. Students improvise the scene without using the script. They may remember lines from the script but are encouraged to change or add lines to present the situation between the scene. Challenge the students to present the scene in two minutes, encouraging them to add dialogue beyond Andrew Moodie's scripted scene.

Responding to a Picture Book

Title of Book: _____

I learned . . .

I wondered . . .

I felt . . .

I remember . . .

Something I would say to the main character:

Turn the sheet over and create an illustration that would show this character sometime in the future (in one year, as a teenager, or as an adult).

Pembroke Publishers © 2020 *Teaching Tough Topics* by Larry Swartz   ISBN 978-1-55138-341-5

Jake's Progress by Andrew Moodie: Excerpt

TERRI: What are you doing?

JAKE: Yeah, listen, I need you to do me a favour.

TERRI: If it has to do with ignoring you, I'm already there!

JAKE: Mrs. Craig told me that I have to take all this stuff about the class project to Pat's house.

TERRI: I thought s/he was still in the hospital.

JAKE: He got out yesterday.

TERRI: And?

JAKE: And???? The guy has TWO DADS! That's what!

TERRI: So he's got a dad and a stepdad. Big deal.

JAKE: Dude, I'm not talking about a stepdad!!!! I'm talking about a dad dad.

TERRI: Dad dad? What's that supposed to mean?

JAKE: Dude pay attention. He's got a dad.

TERRI: Yeah.

JAKE: And he's got another dad.

TERRI: Yeah.

JAKE: And both dads live in the same house. At the same time. No moms. Just dads.

TERRI: No mom?

JAKE: Just dads.

TERRI: OH, Pat's got two dads.

JAKE: SOOOOO?

TERRI: So he's got two dads. So what?

JAKE: You're not supposed to have two dads. You're supposed to have a mom and a dad.

TERRI: I don't have a dad.

JAKE: Well yeah, but . . .

Pembroke Publishers © 2020 *Teaching Tough Topics* by Larry Swartz   ISBN 978-1-55138-341-5

Responding to *Jake's Progress* to Understand Homophobia

Students have opportunities to discuss concepts, improvise conversations, and develop and rehearse a short script of their own.

• *Discussing Homophobia*

Students, working in groups of three or four, share personal definitions and perceptions using the following questions to guide their discussion:

- What is homophobia?
- What is heterosexism?
- What are some reasons why people might be homophobic?
- Do you think it is possible for someone who is homophobic to change? Why or why not?
- Why is homophobia dangerous?
- How might someone with an attitude like Jake's make "progress" in their homophobic beliefs?

• *Improvising a Conversation*

Suppose that Jake's parents learn that Jake was reluctant to deliver the class project material to one of his classmates. Invite students to work in pairs or groups of three to improvise a conversation that Jake might have with his mother, his father, or both parents. What might Jake tell his parent(s)? What questions might the parent(s) ask Jake? What advice could they give Jake?

• *Writing and Presenting a Script*

The script on page 127 is an excerpt from the opening scene of the play where the characters of Jake and Terri have a conversation. As the play unfolds, playwright Andrew Moodie introduces other characters (Chen, Faheen, and Pat). Students can work in pairs or groups of three to create a short script (15 to 20 lines) that shows the conversation Jake or Terri might have with another character. To prepare to write this scene, students may choose to improvise the conversation between Jake or Terri and the other character. This improvised dialogue can help them to write a script. Here are some possible character matchings:

Terri and Mrs. Craig (teacher)	Terri and Pat's father
Jake and Pat	Jake and another friend (Chen, Faheen)
Jake and his mother and father	

Once students have completed their written script, they can work in pairs or groups of three to read the script aloud. Tell students to take turns practising the parts of the different characters. Students can then rehearse how the script might be presented on a stage to an audience.

Here is an example of how two Grade 8 students continued the script:

TERRI: You know it's really OK with me if Pat has two dads.
JAKE: It weirds me out.
TERRI: I'm not sure why, but you still have to give him the work for the class project.
JAKE: Can't you just do this for me? I'll owe you.
TERRI: I don't think Mrs. Craig would like that. There must be a reason she chose you.
JAKE: Fine. I'll go. But will you at least come with me?
TERRI: Sure. I'll go with you, but you are doing all the talking.
JAKE: We'll see about that. What if I have to speak to one of the dads?
TERRI: Dude, don't worry. They're just human beings.

You may want to have students work in groups of five to interpret the full five-page script of *Jake's Progress* as it appears in the resource *More Than a Play*.

JAKE: Yeah, weird human beings.

TERRI: Trust me, they're not weird. Where's this coming from anyway?

JAKE: Let's just go!

Each group, in turn, can present their rehearsed scene to others to learn how Jake made "progress" (or not).

• Writing in Role — Sending an Email Message

Students can imagine that they are one of Jake's classmates. Invite students to write an email message to Jake expressing their thoughts and giving him advice about his behavior. How might they challenge Jake about the things he says or does? What questions might they ask him? What actions would they recommend that Jake take to confront his attitude?

As a follow-up, students can exchange email messages with a partner and write back in the character voice of Jake.

Great Books for a Tough Topic

From *The Princess Boy* by Cheryl Kilodavis

"If you see a Princess Boy . . .
  Will you laugh at him?
  Will you call him a name?
  Will you play with him?
  Will you like him for who he is?"

Picture Books — Gender Roles

Austrian, J. J. (illus. Mike Curato). *Worm Loves Worm*

Baldacchino, Christine (illus. Isabelle Malenfant). *Morris Micklewhite and the Tangerine Dress*

Cole, Babette. *Princess Smartypants*

dePaola, Tomie. *Oliver Button Is a Sissy*

Ewert, Marcus (illus. Rex Ray). *10,000 Dresses*

Gale, Heather (illus. Mika Song). *Hoʻonani: Hula Warrior*

Fullerton, Alma (illus. Renné Benoit). *Hand over Hand*

Herthel, Jessica, and Jazz Jennings (illus. Shelagh McNicholas). *I Am Jazz*

Hoffman, Sarah, and Ian Hoffman (illus. Chris Case). *Jacob's New Dress*

Kilodavis, Cheryl (illus. Suzanne DeSimone). *My Princess Boy*

Love, Jessica. *Julián Is a Mermaid*

Newman, Lesléa (illus. Maria Mola). *Sparkle Boy*

Pessin-Whedbee, Brook (illus. Naomi Bardoff). *Who Are You? The Kid's Guide to Gender Identity* (nonfiction)

Polacco, Patricia. *In Our Mothers' House*

Scotto, Thomas (illus. Olivier Tallec; trans. Claudia Bedrick). *Jerome by Heart*

Setterington, Ken (illus. Alice Priestley). *Mom and Mum Are Getting Married!*

Shraya, Vivek (illus. Rajini Perera). *The Boy & the Bindi*

Silverman, Erica (illus. Holly Hatam). *Jack (Not Jackie)*

Smith, Heather (illus. Brooke Kerrigan). *A Plan for Pops*

Stevenson, Robin. *Ghost's Journey: A Refugee Story*

Zolotow, Charlotte (illus. William Pène du Bois). *William's Doll*

Novels — Gender Roles

Cassidy, Sara. *A Boy Named Queen*

Gino, Alex. *George*

Fine, Anne (illus. Philippe Dupasquier). *Bill's New Frock*

Hennessey, M. G. *The Other Boy*

Howe, James. *Totally Joe*

Tilson, Sonia. *The Disappearing Boy*

Influential Series

In 2007, J. K. Rowling, of Harry Potter fame, announced that the wizard Dumbledore was gay. As for his Captain Underpants series, Dav Pilkey has quietly revealed that Harold, one of the two main characters, grows up to marry a man. The news about these well-known characters can be considered a big step forward in children literature and could prove useful in promoting acceptance of differences, even more so than books centred on gay children and parents.

Walliams, David. *The Boy in the Dress*
Wang, Jen. *The Prince and the Dressmaker*

Novels — Homosexuality and Homophobia

Blake, Ashley Herring. *Ivy Aberdeen's Letter to the World*
Callender, Kheryn. *Hurricane Child*
Donoghue, Emma. *The Lotterys Plus One*
Gephart, Donna. *Lily and Dunkin*
Hitchcock, Shannon. *One True Way*
Huser, Glen. *Stitches*
Melleby, Nicole. *Hurricane Season*
Peck, Richard. *The Best Man*

Young Adult — Coming Out, Overcoming Homophobia, and Gender Identity

Albertalli, Becky, and Adam Silvera. *What If It's Us*
Beam, Cris. *I Am J*
Belge, Kathy, and Marke Bieschke. *Queer: The Ultimate LGBT Guide for Teens* (nonfiction)
Boyne, John. *My Brother's Name Is Jessica*
Clark, Kristin Elizabeth. *Freakboy*
Cronn-Mills, Kirstin. *Beautiful Music for Ugly Children*
Ellis, Deborah. *Moon at Nine*
Emezi, Akwaeke. *Pet*
Henstra, Sarah. *We Contain Multitudes*
Jones, Adam Garnet. *Fire Song*
Liang, Bridget. *What Makes You Beautiful*
Newman, Lesléa. *October Mourning: A Song for Matthew Shepard* (poetry)
Nielsen, Susin. *We Are All Made of Molecules*
Pearson, Kit. *Be My Love*
Peters, Julie Anne. *Luna*
Polonsky, Ami. *Gracefully Grayson*
Russo, Meredith. *Birthday*
Sáenz, Benjamin Alire. *Aristotle and Dante Discover the Secrets of the Universe*
Savage, Dan, and Terry Miller, eds. *It Gets Better: Coming Out, Overcoming Bullying, and Creating a Life Worth Living* (nonfiction)
Smedley, Zack. *Deposing Nathan*
Tamaki, Mariko (illus. Valero-O'Connell, Rosemary). *Laura Dean Keeps Breaking Up with Me* (graphic novel)
Williamson, Lisa. *The Art of Being Normal*
Wittlinger, Ellen. *Parrotfish*

Chapter 9

Bullying

Don't laugh at me.
Don't call me names.
Don't get your pleasure from my pain.

— From *Don't Laugh at Me* by Steve Seskin and Allen Shamblin, illustrated by Glin Dibley

everything bad and frightening and loud
will always hide when you hold your head up,
will always hide when you hold your heart out,
will always sing a shrinking song
when you fly.

— From "A Talkin'-To" by Jason Reynolds, in *We Rise, We Resist, We Raise Our Voices*, compiled by Wade Hudson and Cheryl Willis Hudson

Sticks and stones may break my bones,
But words can also hurt me.
Stones and sticks break only skin,
While words are ghosts that haunt me.

— From "The Truth" by Barrie Wade

When I was a Grade 4 teacher, there was an ongoing incident of a Grade 6 "mean girl" who was manipulative and cruel to others. The students in my class told me about this, with some students expressing their anxieties. The school staff quickly became aware of the situation and intervened. The bullying seemed to stop (at least in the school environment).

Taking Action on Bullying

If I can stop one heart from breaking,
I shall not live in vain;
If I can ease one life the aching,
Or cool one pain,
Or help one fainting robin
Unto his nest again,
I shall not live in vain.

— Emily Dickinson

I recognized a need to discuss the bully issue with my students. In the classroom, I turned to what is now considered an early children's literature title dealing with the topic of bullying: *Thank You, Mr. Falker* by Patricia Polacco. This picture book tells the autobiographical story of a young girl who was bullied because of her learning disability and a special teacher who helps her to conquer her fears and have faith in herself. Through fiction and through discussion, I helped the students consider the *who what where when why* and *how* of bullying incidents.

This book was but one story. Although no curriculum document guides us to "teach bullying," I felt that there was a need to go further in my teaching. For the next three weeks, I developed integrated reading, writing, talk, and arts activities that helped to bring attention to bullying. Each book I introduced served as a case study to examine the issue and help students understand why a bully behaves the way he or she does and what strategies need to be considered to handle bullies. In some way, I believe, this unit served as an antidote to the fears and experiences of my young students.

Caring Classrooms: Taking a Literacy Approach

Creating Caring Classrooms by Kathleen Gould Lundy and Larry Swartz focuses on the 5 Cs, as reflected in its chapter titles: Community, Communication, Collaboration, Compassion, and Confronting the Bully Issue (for which there are 12 lessons).

Bullying is pervasive. Media are rife with reports of it. Many people find the problem inescapable.

In the past 10 years, I have intentionally included the topic of bullying in my literacy and drama classes in the teacher education program at the Ontario Institute for Studies in Education (OISE). I have also been invited to present more than 50 workshops on the topic of bullying throughout the province and in Beijing, Auckland, Vienna, Jordan, and Cairo. The title of the session is "Creating Caring Classrooms: A Literacy Approach to Bullying." One of my main goals is to help teachers understand that we need to build a community, provide contexts for communication and collaboration, and introduce children's literature that builds compassion; then, we can work towards understanding and dealing with those caught in the bully web, including the triangle of bully, bullied, and bystander.

Children's Literature as Case Studies

Today, most young readers who choose to read fiction will encounter characters who are stressed out by the mean treatment of others. I would say that over 50 percent of realistic fiction for children ages 8 through 13 will find a character who is being teased, taunted, or tormented by others. Students can learn about their own sense of belonging by reading about the trials and tribulations of Auggie Pullman in *Wonder* by R. J. Palacio, Donald Zinkoff in *Loser* by Jerry Spinelli, Shannon in *Real Friends* by Shannon Hale and LeUyen Pham, Annabelle in *Wolf Hollow* by Lauren Wolk, and Will Reid in *Egghead* by Caroline Pignat.

We need to find space, or a kind of forum, in the curriculum to help students dig deeply into understanding that everyone has the right to respect. We also need to introduce stories in novels, picture books, and poetry, as well as in the media, films, and YouTube selections, that invite written, oral, and dramatic responses; these will allow students to make connections and consider strategies for dealing with difficult relationships.

Fiction and nonfiction sources can provide contexts that allow us to share ideas and responses. Each piece of literature we offer about bullying presents a case study of a situation that can help our students stand up for themselves and act with integrity while learning to respect the rights and needs of others and handle conflict nonviolently.

In *Making a Difference in Bullying*, Debra Peplar and Wendy Craig (2000, 10) provide an intriguing statistic from their research:

"71% of teachers and 25% of students say that teachers almost always intervene."

Relationship Solutions Required

According to researcher Debra Peplar, bullying is a relationship problem and needs relationship solutions. In our classrooms, we need to create social contexts that promote positive interactions. When we build a strong community, provide authentic contexts for students to communicate and collaborate with one another — and introduce children's literature that builds empathy — we are providing meaningful programming.

Every teacher, every parent, and every student would expect and hope that classrooms are safe places for all. Teachers may have some control about what happens between 9:00 a.m. and 3:30 p.m. within the classroom walls, but students live and play outside the classroom, outside the school building.

The work we do with bullying is about enriching relationships and we can guide students into making moral, ethical choices about their treatment of others. They can learn about respect in a community that thrives on respect. They can learn about tolerance, acceptance, compassion, and empathy in the classroom: principles that are central to social justice, equity, and diversity and essential to being caring citizens of the world.

The Bully Issue Beyond the Classroom

About 60 percent of students admit that someone has said or done something mean to them online; about 50 percent claim that it has happened more than once.

— i-Safe America

"Everyone failed my son," mother says after boy, 14, fatally stabbed at Hamilton school.
— *Toronto Star*, Thursday, October 10, 2019

Bullies are present not only on playgrounds and in cyberspace, picture books, novels, and poems, but also in posters, movies, television shows, news reports, and politics. Is bullying a normal way of life? Will bullying ever stop? What happens when bullying incidents are ignored? Will there ever be a day when the word *bully* does not appear in our media headlines?

Too many young people keep inside themselves stories about being involved in a bullying incident because they lack the courage to let others know what is happening to them. Many other young people have been bullied and have told others of what has happened to them, but their stories have not been well resolved. Such was the case for Hamilton, Ontario, student Devan Bracci-Selvey, who was continually bullied by two boys and killed by one of them on October 7, 2019.

Attention must be paid! Drawing on a wealth of children's literature that exposes and illuminates the issue is one way to give it.

The Language and Vocabulary of Bullying

"Opinionnaire: What Are Your Views of Bullying?" is designed to help students in Grades 4 to 9 in two ways: (1) to explore vocabulary connected to the topic of bullying (Parts A and B) and (2) to share their assumptions about bullying (Part C), which can serve as an Opening Up activity. See the line master on page 135. (Teachers of younger students may want to choose statements from the line master and present them to the class for discussion.)

An *Opinionnaire*, a kind of questionnaire, is a strategy that allows students to share what they think about a given topic. Students are encouraged to consider and record their opinions spontaneously, using a scale. Some students may be unsure of what to think about an item, however, and can answer "unsure." It is important to remind students that completing items will help them to consider their opinions and assumptions — they need not think in terms of being right or wrong. Essentially, student answers are dependent on their experiences.

Most words on the Part B list *are* synonyms for the verb *bullying*. For example, *taunting* and *harassing* appropriately describe much of bullying behavior. Although bullies may *argue* with someone, arguing is not necessarily restricted to bullying. Vocabulary items may be explained either before or after students complete this activity.

- Part A — *Making sense.* Instruct students to fill in each sentence blank with a word that they think is most appropriate.
- Part B — *Considering synonyms.* Students read the list of 21 words and consider which ones serve as synonyms for the word *bullying*. Answers will vary.
- Part C — *Considering opinions.* Students respond to each statement by checking whether they strongly agree, agree, feel unsure, disagree, or strongly disagree. You may want to have them complete Part C later, once you move on to Opening Up the Topic of Bullying.

Kinds of Bullying

The most obvious kind of bullying is the situation where at least one person exerts power or threat over another in the presence of others; however, there are at least two more bullying scenarios, not to be overlooked in any exploration of this tough topic.

- **Face-to-face bullying** involves someone acting aggressively against someone else in the same physical environment. The bullying can be physical or verbal.
  - *Physical bullying* is a visible form of bullying that includes harmful acts, such as slapping, hitting, poking, punching, kicking, scratching, and spitting.
  - *Verbal bullying* involves using words as put-downs to break the spirit of a child who is on the receiving end. It is the most common form of bullying for both boys and girls of all ages.

If not addressed, the bullying may happen repeatedly. The presence of a bystander may turn the relationship into a bully triangle.

- **Indirect, or relational, bullying** is harder to detect than face-to-face bullying but can cause much emotional harm. Barbara Coloroso (2003, 17) defines it as "the systematic diminishment of a bullied child's sense of self through ignoring, isolating, excluding, or shunning."
- **Cyberbullying** takes place over digital devices such as cell phones, computers, and tablets. It includes sending, posting, or sharing negative, harmful, false, or mean content about someone else. Sharing private information about another person in a public forum can cause embarrassment or humiliation. Some cyberbullying constitutes unlawful or criminal behavior.

What Are You?

"Bystanders" and "upstanders" are two related concepts. In the traditional bully triangle, a bystander is the third party, the spectator, the witness to the bullying incident. Depending on whether bystanders become involved or not, they can either be part of the problem or part of the solution. Upstanders are individuals who recognize bullying as wrong and act to make a given situation right — they strive to give support to and protect the bullied.

In the Afterword to his novel *My Brother's Name Is Jessica*, John Boyne writes: "It's hard to stand up for those who are already being victimized because to throw in our lot with them can make us a target too. But if we don't stand up for the oppressed, then one way or another we become the oppressors. If we don't stand side by side with the bullied, then we are complicit in the bullying. So, pick a side. Choose the kind of person you want to be. And be able to live with that decision."

Opening Up the Topic of Bullying

The topic of bullying arouses strong emotions and opinions. Use of the Four Corners strategy acknowledges that. Having students fill in "Opinionnaire: What Are Your Views of Bullying?" — a tool designed to elicit opinions and perhaps expose flaws in thinking — can also be part of this exploration.

Four Corners — Which One Will You Choose?

Four Corners is a cooperative learning activity that encourages participants to express a point of view, share it with others, and listen to the revealed opinions, some of which may be different from their own. It can be repeated three or four times, with the teacher providing different statements to respond to.

1. The following words are posted on four signs, one in each of the four corners of a room: **Strongly Agree, Agree, Disagree, Strongly Disagree**. Letting students indicate that they are unsure about a statement is also an option. Those who feel unsure can stand in the centre of the room.

Opinionnaire: What Are Your Views of Bullying?

Part A: Fill in the blank with the word that seems most appropriate. Answers will vary.

1. Someone who is being bullied is a _____ (*target, coward, nerd*).
2. Bullying is a _____ ongoing hostile activity. (*deliberate, common, violent*)
3. The opposite of a bystander is _____ (*a hero, an upstander, a witness*).
4. When adults bully each other, it is thought to be _____
   (*harassment, a power issue, argument*).
5. Cyberbullying can often be _____ (*private, anonymous, social*).
6. One word I would use to describe a bully is _____ .
7. One word I would use to describe someone who is bullied is _____ .

Part B: Circle any words you think are **NOT** a synonym for the word *bullying*.

intimidating	pestering	taunting	annoying	fighting	pressuring	forcing
coercing	bothering	badgering	hassling	aggravating	arguing	tormenting
oppressing	abusing	teasing	attacking	shadowing	hurting	gossiping

Part C: Consider each of these statements. Record whether you Strongly Agree (SA), Agree (A), feel Unsure (U), Disagree (D), or Strongly Disagree with it.

Statement	Level of Agreement
1. Most bullies have friends.	_____
2. Bullies will go away if you ignore them.	_____
3. There are as many boy bullies as girl bullies.	_____
4. The best way to solve a bully problem is to get even.	_____
5. Cyberbullying mostly happens outside school — it is not a school problem.	_____
6. Cyberbullies go away if no one responds to their messages.	_____
7. Once a bully, always a bully.	_____
8. Bullies generally think poorly about themselves.	_____
9. The best way to handle bullying is to report the problem to a teacher.	_____
10. Telling someone you've been bullied usually makes things better for you.	_____

Pembroke Publishers © 2020 *Teaching Tough Topics* by Larry Swartz   ISBN 978-1-55138-341-5

You can either have students contemplate the line-master statements first or have them respond to the statements afterwards.

2. Offer students a statement that invites them to think about bullying. You can choose from statements on the line master, such as these:
   - Bullies will go away if you ignore them.
   - The best way to solve a bully problem is to get even.
   - Cyberbullying mostly happens outside of school — it is not a school problem.
3. Students then move to the corner of the room that designates their opinions. Once students of similar mind meet, they can share their views with others, giving reasons for their choices. Unsure students in the centre of the room also talk together.
4. Volunteers from each of the five groups can then share their opinions with the whole class.

General Extensions for the Opinionnaire

1. Once students have completed the Opinionnaire, invite them to work in small groups where students hold different views to share their opinions. Encourage students to give reasons for their choices.
2. Facilitate a discussion with the whole class. Doing this is a meaningful way for students to reveal and challenge assumptions; it is also a way for them to come closer to understanding the issue by making connections based on their experiences.

Model Lesson 1: Writing from a Character's Perspective

This lesson works well for students in Grades 3 to 9.

Character Journals, a type of perspective writing, is a strategy that can be introduced with almost any theme in *Teaching Tough Topics*. By becoming an "other," by retelling events from a book, and by reflecting on and expressing a character's life, students come to a better understanding of the life of that character.

Depending on the source picture book, novel, poem, or nonfiction story, students can journey into the world of someone experiencing poverty, racism, homophobia, or other such matters related to social justice, equity, and diversity. They might empathize with the character or they might imagine that they *are* the character.

Featured Text: Say Something *by Peggy Moss, illustrated by Lea Lyon, or* Dear Bully of Mine *by Vicki Fraser, illustrated by Cody and Sean McGrath*

Writing a journal entry from a character's perspective enables the reader to have a conversation with the text, giving the reader as much responsibility as the author in the making of meaning. Character Journals is a strategy that integrates reading, writing, and talk — it ignites personal response to a text. The character created by the author becomes very real for the students as they take on that character's perspective.

It can be somewhat of a challenge to teach the students about voice in writing; however, when they become the *I* in the story through a fictitious journal entry, they are, indeed, exploring voice. Students, through retelling, are determining important events and issues of the story; they are also making inferences about those issues and events and reflecting on the problems as a character in the story might experience them.

In the Character of a Bully, a Target, or a Bystander

The Character Journal activity can be introduced as students engage with fiction, nonfiction, and poetry connected to this topic (see Great Books for a Tough Topic, page 143). Individual students can either respond to books they have chosen to read independently, or the whole class can respond to the same source. Two specific picture book excerpts are offered for possible use below.

The following excerpts can be used as sources for exploring Character Journals. In the first, students can choose to be a bully, the bullied, or a bystander to express their reactions to the incident from *Say Something* by Peggy Moss, illustrated by Lea Lyon:

Because students are encouraged to express ideas in an open-ended way, are moving into the world of *as if*, and can draw on story events to motivate them, they find that perspective writing is a rich, viable way of making a book report.

A girl who rides on my bus
Always sits alone.
Sometimes kids throw things at her and call her names.
The girls who sit behind her laugh.
I don't laugh.
I don't say anything.

Another picture book, *Dear Bully of Mine* by Vicki Fraser, illustrated by Cody and Sean McGrath, digs deeply into the feelings and internal battle of three children who are being targeted. Writing a letter to the bullies provides a context for those who are bullied to raise their voices and question the power of those who have harassed them. Here is an excerpt of first-person letter writing:

You choose your words like weapons.
They stab me like a knife,
Break my spirit,
Tear me down,
Slowly
Ruin
My
Life

Motivating Perspective Writing: Tips

- A good time to implement the in-role activity is after an independent reading time. Students can retell in role something that happened in the book they read.
- Give students the choice of writing a journal entry about a single event in the book or a series of events over time.
- Tell students that their entries may be written from the point of view of an animal or an inanimate object.
- Let students choose how to write their entries: by hand or on the computer.
- Invite students to consider what might be an appropriate format, kind of paper, and font to bring authenticity to the writing.
- Suggest that creating illustrations or graphics for the entry is an option.

In this sample of perspective writing, Grade 7 student Sophie T. "becomes" Auggie Pullman from the novel *Wonder* by R. J. Palacio. She creates a moving diary entry from the character's point of view, revealing anxieties and thoughts about being teased and tormented by others.

Dear Diary,

Today in class, Mr. Brown wrote another one of his precepts on the whiteboard: "In the choice of being kind or right, choose kind." I thought to myself, "if it's such an easy decision to be kind, why doesn't it just come naturally to everyone?" I'd like to say, after being in the school for a while now, that the remarks, giggles, and looks I get don't bother me. Unfortunately, that's not the case. Every day I get unusual stares from the crossing guard and the lady who works at the supermarket. Other people, including the students in my school, just do that "look away thing" and I think that hurts more.

And then there's Julian, who never seems to pick on anybody but me. I once confronted him and asked why he always gives me such unwanted attention. He told me that it's because when he sees me, I bring his nightmares back. Nightmares? Mom always tells me that I have a big heart because I always look for the best in people. However, in this situation, I don't know if I can give Julian the benefit of the doubt. I have told him many many times that when he bullies me, I feel broken down, but that never seems to stop him.

I decided to tell Mom about Julian, but by the way she acted, it didn't seem like there was much that she could do. Mom told me to focus on the things that give me comfort like my astronaut helmet and my Padawan braid. I try to stick to mom's advice, but a couple of weeks ago, Mr. Brown made me and Julian partner up for our class project. I know that Mr. Brown was only trying to help, but I think that he did more damage than good. Julian told me that he didn't want us to work together and even said that "if he looked like me, he would kill himself." The second he said that it felt like my stomach had dropped to my knees. I wanted to throw up. I couldn't imagine how anyone could be so cruel. Why would he say something like that?

I hope that Julian can find something that makes him happy so that I don't have to suffer the consequences of his sadness. I know that I don't look like an average ten-year-old, but there's nothing that I can do about that. Don't bullies understand that? I just hope that people can give me a chance to let me just be myself before they judge me. Just like Mr. Brown's precept says: I hope they choose kindness.

Sincerely,
Me (Auggie)

Improvised In-Role Conversations

An important follow-up to the writing assignment is to have the students share their responses with each other by working in role. Students work in pairs, with one person (partner A) first silently reading their partner's writing. Partner A then interviews partner B, who speaks in role as a character. Partners repeat the activity, with roles reversed, so that each person has a chance to be interviewed. In this way, the activity promotes a talk response to the reading and writing experience, while it initiates drama exploration.

Additional Contexts for Perspective Writing on Bullying

When exploring this topic, there are essentially three identities for students to consider: the bully, the bullied, or the bystander. Perspective writing in various contexts can help students step into the shoes of a character and thus build understanding of that character by writing in the first person. Beyond having students write a journal entry from the point of view of a character, invite them to use their imaginations and write any of the following in character:

- a letter of advice from one character in the book to another, perhaps a child being bullied or someone wondering about whether to intervene or not

- a letter to a local or school newspaper advice columnist, someone considered an "expert," from a character being bullied and feeling trapped or perhaps from a concerned parent (Students, in pairs, could exchange letters and write back as the columnist offering ways to handle the problem.)
- an email from one character to another, possibly about a bullying incident witnessed or experiences of being bullied
- a character's post on a Facebook wall, perhaps a plea for help and support to deal with a bully
- a first-hand newspaper, magazine, or media account of an incident derived from the story
- a series of text messages between two characters; for example, between someone who has been bullied and someone sought out for advice, between a bystander and a bullied, or between a bystander and a bully

---

Text-Message Conversations

This activity allows students working in pairs to focus on character and plot while drawing on technology and media literacy to make inferences.

Students select an important or pivotal moment in a book and create an imaginary text-message conversation between two characters from the book. The conversation might describe or comment on the significant event. Alternatively, as characters from two different books that were chosen for independent reading, students could interact via text-messaging.

Invite students to consider their own text-message conversations so that they duplicate their style and form. Remind students to consider the way the character would text, using vocabulary and expressions as that character would.

Extensions

- Students work in pairs to read their conversations aloud and share with the class, thereby giving the class a sense of the characters.
- Students dramatize this scripted conversation as if it were a scene in a play.
- Students extend the text-message conversation by improvising a dialogue between the two characters.

Model Lesson 2: Interpreting Poems Through Choral Dramatization

Featured Texts: See the selection of poems on the line master titled "Poems on Bullying." These poems appear in The Bully, the Bullied, the Bystander, the Brave, *collected by David Booth and Larry Swartz.*

This lesson works well with students in Grades 3 to 9.

Choral dramatization invites students to read aloud such texts as rhymes and poems by assigning parts among group members. By working with peers to read aloud poems on a certain theme or topic, or by a single poet, students take part in a creative, collaborative activity that involves experimentation with voice, sound, gesture, and movement. Because of these variations, no two oral interpretations of a single poem are alike.

When we read a poem on a page, it can be little more than black ink on white paper. When we read the poem aloud, we are animating print, making it come to life through our voices. As students explore choral dramatization and consider how best to interpret a poem, they are helping to illuminate the poem's meaning.

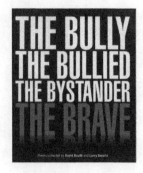

When done well, interpretation improves comprehension skills, enabling students, both interpreters and listeners, to appreciate much of the meaning to which the words give rise.

The poetry on page 141 can be used as a source for choral dramatization. These poems appear in the anthology *The Bully, the Bullied, the Bystander, the Brave.* Through choral dramatization, students can work collaboratively to dig deeper into the stories, the relationships, and the emotions conveyed by the poets' words about the bully issue.

How to Interpret Bully Poems Aloud

The following outline can guide the students in planning, rehearsing, and presenting a choral dramatization of bully poems.

1. Students work together in groups of four or five. Each group is assigned one poem and members are challenged to read it aloud together in a manner of their choice. They might experiment with reading their poem aloud in any of the following ways:
   - as echo reading: A leader says one part; remaining group members repeat or echo the leader.
   - as alternate reading: A leader says one line; remaining group members say alternate lines.
   - in unison: The whole group reads aloud the poem simultaneously.
   - with cloze technique: When a reading leader omits one word (or more), members join in to say the word(s).
   - using assigned parts: Either lines (or parts of lines) are given to individuals or groups.
   - with use of soft and loud voices: Students can experiment with this.
   - with rhythm clapping: It can accompany the reading.
   - through singing: Sometimes a familiar tune can be used for the reading of the poem.
   - as a round
   - with the addition of gestures, movement, and/or sound effects

2. Encourage group members to think about these questions as they develop their interpretations:
   Which lines will we read in unison?
   How will we divide the lines among us?
   What voices will we use to bring meaning to the text?
   What gestures, sounds, and rhythms can we add to our presentation?
   How will we begin and end our presentation?

3. Have the groups agree on and rehearse their interpretations. Once group members are familiar with their parts, they can share their presentation with another group, the whole class, or another class.

Further Ways of Responding to Bully Poems

Students can discuss poems on bullying, illuminate text through illustration, or compose their own poems while referring to the line-master models.

• Discussing the Poems to Explore the Issue

Students first work independently, choosing *one* poem from the line master and responding to it by answering the following.

1. Do you think this poem is about a bully? a bullied? a bystander? Why?

Getting the Message Out

As a further goal, the students could work towards performing the poems at a school concert or assembly.

Poems on Bullying

Those Who Stare But Don't Act*
I dint See Nothing

Cover your eyes,
Cover your ears,
Cover your mouth.
Ignore all the jeers.

Run from the playground
Run through the door,
Leave them behind,
You've been there before.

Mind your own business,
Mind what you say,
Don't get involved
It's safer that way.

Finding the Blue*
I was walking home from school
Down Yonge Street with my dad,
Saddened by my day,
Saddened by my classmates,
By their savage conversations
About the others — the outsiders, the
    outliers,
Those who are always the others
No matter who they are
No matter who they will become.

Suddenly my dad said: "Look up!
You can see the lake and the skyline."
I'd been looking down,
Trapped by the pavement,
By the feet stomping on my life.
Now there it was — the lake.
Between the cement forests,
Blue, level, constant.

"Teach me to look up, Dad,"
I should have said.
But I didn't. Sons don't.
He always looks up —
Past the anonymous faces,
Past the gas-fuelled traffic,
Past the hurt from his day,
Because that is the only way
To see the lake ahead.

And to dream of the kayak
That will carry me away
Into the blue…
Where I will be
Inside and outside

All at once.

Bird Food*
Seven huge ravens
Roost in that tree
Sharp-beaked birds
Staring at me.

I sit on this bench
Every day
Afraid to move,
On display.

Am I waiting for them?
Are they waiting for me?
Break the spell,
Set us free.

Mosquito\+
She's tiny.
She's mean.
She's cruel.
She fights.

The mosquito
Buzzes.
The mosquito
Bites.

She torments.
She swarms.
She teases.
She taunts.

The mosquito
Buzzes.
The mosquito
Haunts.

You're bigger than her.
Your blood is what feeds.
Beware of the bully —
You're the victim she needs.

After Words\+
I will not be a bystander
I will not be a bystander
I will not be a bystander
I will not be a bystander
I will not be a bystander
I will not be a bystander
I will not
I will not be
I will not bystand
I will not stand by
I will not stand
I will stand
I will stand by her
I will stand by her
I will

Standing By\+
I don't know why
I just stood by
When she started to cry.

If I were to cry,
Would she just stand by
Or would she stand up for me
Like a good friend would?
Could?
(Should?)

Bully for You\+
You wouldn't know it by looking at
    him.
You wouldn't know it by his clothes.
But inside he knows you laughed at
    him.
He's the victim that nobody knows.

You wouldn't know it by looking at
    him.
You wouldn't know it by his clothes.
But inside he knows how he made you
    feel.
He's the bully that everybody knows.

Giggles and Whispers\+
See that giggling girl
Over there with the crowd
(standing far away from me)
I wish we were friends.
(We used to be.)
We talked
Told secrets,
Laughed.
We once whispered the names of
    those
Who we wanted as our friends.

One day
Like the *snap* of a finger
She stopped liking me.
Left me
Alone
(as if I had done something wrong).
Does she remember
When we told secrets and talked and
    laughed?
(It wasn't that long ago.)

Does she remember when we once
Whispered
The names of those
Who we wanted as our friends?

These poems appear in *The Bully, the Bullied, the Bystander, the Brave*, collected by David Booth and Larry Swartz (Oakville, ON: Rubicon, 2013). * signifies a poem by David Booth; \+ signifies a poem by Larry Swartz.

Pembroke Publishers © 2020 *Teaching Tough Topics* by Larry Swartz   ISBN 978-1-55138-341-5

2. Underline a snippet — a fragment or excerpt — from the poem that interests you. It may be words that create a strong image or highlight the poem's theme.
3. Complete the following thinking stem: "I wonder . . ." What questions or matters of curiosity come to mind when reading this poem?

Students then work in groups of three or four with others who have focused on a poem different from theirs. They share their written responses to the poem, considering questions like these:

- How are the poems similar or different?
- What do you think the poet is saying about bullying?
- Does the poem remind you of bully situations you have heard or read about in the news, read about in books, or seen in plays? How?

• Illustrating Poem Texts

Tell the students to imagine that they have been asked to illustrate a poem for an anthology of bully poems. Choice of poem is up to them. It might be one from the line master, found on the Internet, or written by the student. Students then choose a medium such as markers, paint, charcoal, torn paper, or collage, to create a visual image to accompany the text. If desired, they can include figures in their illustration or create an abstract design representing ideas in the poem.

Once their work is completed, the class can assemble their poems with illustrations into an anthology of bully poetry.

• Writing Poems About Bullying

Students can create a poem about a bully, a bullied, or a bystander. Encourage students to use one of the poems on the line master "Poems on Bullying" as a model for their writing. Students tend to create poems using a rhyme scheme; however, you may want to recommend that they present their poems as free verse: finding a suitable rhythm and rhyme pattern can be challenging for them.

Here are two suggestions for writing poems:

Creature Bully Poems. "Mosquito" by Larry Swartz (see the line master) can serve as a suitable model. To begin, tell the students that they are going to write a poem about a bully or someone who is being bullied. The poem is going to feature a creature of their choice (e.g., a mouse, a fox, a bear, a shark). Ask:

- What creature would you choose to represent either a bully or someone who is bullied?
- How would you describe the creature's appearance? the creature's actions?
- What behaviors of this creature would identify it as a bully or as a bullied?

Tell students to write a sentence or two about how this creature is like a bully or someone who is bullied. Encourage them to use words, phrases, and facts about the creature. They can then transform this sentence into a free verse poem by writing one, two, or three words on a single line.

Free Verse Poems from Snippets. Students choose at least one snippet or fragment from a poem that appears on the line master. They then add their own thoughts about what happened before, after, or before and after the fragment. Students manipulate the words they have written into a free verse poem by writing one, two, or three words on a single line.

Once students have composed their poems, the poems can be displayed in the classroom or in a class blog or gathered into a class anthology of bully poems.

On one occasion, when I engaged Grade 3 students in writing bully poems with animal characters, they chose creatures ranging from lions, tigers, and sharks to Tyrannosaurus rex and the Minotaur.

A Creature Bully Poem

I am
the cheetah.
I am
a
 fast
   fast
animal.
I hunt people down.
It's hard
to escape
 from
     me!

The line master "Responding to a Poem" provides several thought-eliciting questions and directions that can help students focus on the bully poems. By responding to each of these questions, students reveal their comprehension of a poem; they can make connections, share their questions, visualize, and so on.

Great Books for a Tough Topic

Over the years, I have collected more than 300 children's literature titles on the topic of bullying. These include picture books for the teacher to read aloud, chapter books, novels for both middle-year students and Young Adults, reference books for students, teachers, and parents, and films and documentaries.

Picture Books

Baldacchino, Christine (illus. Isabelle Malenfant). *Morris Micklewhite and the Tangerine Dress*
Choi, Yangsook. *The Name Jar*
Falcone, Lucy M. (illus. Jacqueline Hudon). *I Didn't Stand Up*
Hughes, Susan (illus. Carey Sookocheff). *What Happens Next*
Ludwig, Trudy (illus. Beth Adams). *Confessions of a Former Bully*
Moss, Peggy (illus. Lea Lyon). *Say Something*
Otoshi, Kathryn. *One*
Polacco, Patricia. *Bully*
———. *Thank You, Mr. Falker*
Reynolds, Peter H. *Say Something!*
Rosenberg, Liz (illus. Stephen Gammell). *Monster Mama*
Seskin, Steve, and Allen Shamblin (illus. Glin Dibley). *Don't Laugh at Me*
Woodson, Jacqueline (illus. E. B Lewis). *Each Kindness*

Novels

Anderson, John David. *Posted*
Baron, Chris. *All of Me*
Blume, Judy. *Blubber*
Estes, Eleanor (illus. Louis Slobodkin). *The Hundred Dresses*
Hale, Shannon (illus. LeUyen Pham). *Real Friends*
Howe, James. *The Misfits*
Kerz, Anna. *Better Than Weird*
Levy, Dana Alison. *It Wasn't Me* (YA)
Nielsen, Susin. *The Reluctant Journal of Henry K. Larsen*
Palacio, R. J. *Wonder*
Paterson, Katherine (illus. Emily Arnold McCully). *The Field of the Dogs*
Patterson, James, and Chris Grabenstein (illus. Stephen Gilpin). *Pottymouth and Stoopid*
Pignat, Caroline. *Egghead*
Sher, Emil (photographer David Wyman). *Young Man with Camera*
Spinelli, Jerry. *Loser* (Also: *Wringer*)
Wolk, Lauren. *Wolf Hollow* (YA)

Other

Booth, David, and Larry Swartz, eds. *The Bully, the Bullied, the Bystander, the Brave* (poetry)
Ellis, Deborah, ed. *We Want You to Know: Kids Talk About Bullying*
Hall, Megan Kelley, and Carrie Jones. *Dear Bully: 70 Authors Tell Their Stories*
Porter, Helen Carmichael. *The Bully and Me: Stories That Break the Cycle of Torment*

Responding to a Poem

1. Describe in one sentence what you think the poem is about.

_____

2. What do you like about the poem?

_____

3. What do you not like about the poem?

_____

4. What did this poem remind you of?

_____

5. What things in this poem did you see? hear? feel?

_____

6. What would you tell or ask the poet about the poem?

_____

7. Identify a snippet, or excerpt, from this poem that you particularly liked.

_____

8. What is an alternative title you would suggest for this poem?

_____

9. Complete this statement: When I read the poem, I wonder . . .

_____

10. On the reverse side of this paper, create an illustration that you think might accompany this poem.

Pembroke Publishers © 2020 *Teaching Tough Topics* by Larry Swartz   ISBN 978-1-55138-341-5

Chapter 10

Ripples of Kindness

We're part of a community.
Our strength is our diversity.
A shelter from adversity.
We are all welcome here.

— From *All Are Welcome* by Alexandra Penfold, illustrated by
Suzanne Kaufman

If you could line up all the people who want to be
good and all the people who want to be bad, the good
line would stretch from here to the tallest mountain.
All the people in the bad line could crowd together in
a dark and gloomy room.

— From *Most People* by Michael Leannah, illustrated by
Jennifer E. Morris

Ms. Albert had brought a big bowl into the class and
filled it with water. We all gathered around her desk
and watched her drop a small stone into it. Tiny
waves rippled out, away from the stone. This is what
kindness does, Ms. Albert said. Each little thing we do
goes out, like a ripple into the world.

— From *Each Kindness* by Jacqueline Woodson, illustrated by
E. B. Lewis

Creating a Culture of Kindness

Jacqueline Woodson is the 2018–2019 National Ambassador for Young People's Literature. *Each Kindness* won the Coretta Scott King Honor Book Award and the Jane Addams Peace Award.

On my website (larryswartz.ca), there appears this banner:

Active Joyful Learning

For me that serves as a personal philosophy.

I believe that students need to be **active** participants in the classroom. They need to help make decisions about routines and they need to abide by a classroom slogan, suggested most often by the teacher and shown as a poster or banner. They need to know that they are actively involved in a safe space where their voices are heard, varied opinions are respected, and they will have interactive experiences in order to enrich social understanding and social growth. Classrooms need to be **joyful**. Humor can promote a comfortable space for learning. Students need to be engaged in the work that they do. Having choice in the **learning** empowers them. When students are successful — and our job is to ensure that each student in our classroom *is* successful — they can feel joy. When students are **active**, when students are **joyful**, they are **learning**.

The more we get together,
Together, together,
The more we get together,
The happier we'll be.

— Traditional

"There are three ways to ultimate success. The first way is to be kind. The second way is to be kind. The third way is to be kind."

— Fred Rogers

In an introduction to *Creating Caring Classrooms*, my colleague Kathleen Gould Lundy writes that caring is such a common-sense, basic thing and teachers need to foster it: "We need to spend time creating a non-competitive culture of listening and cooperation, and an ethic of hearing and valuing everyone's voice. Some teachers might say they don't have time to do this: that it takes too much planning, energy, and time away from the real purpose of education — to teach the curriculum . . . creating this culture *is* the curriculum: that teaching students how to respect one another, value differing opinions, share common experiences, and work towards a critical understanding of complex relationships and ideas is at least partly what school should be about. The goal of an inclusive pedagogy is to create learning environments that reflect, affirm, celebrate, and validate the diversity and complexity of the human experience" (2011, 6).

When a classroom is underpinned by caring, students will be active and joyful — and they will learn. This learning will emerge if we provide a space in which students feel safe with those around them and feel respectful towards them; where, as Ellen DeGeneres tells her TV listeners, they accept the guidance of "be kind to one another."

Eric Walters is author of more than 100 books for young people, and caring and compassion are at the heart of his work. In the feature "Teaching Kindness?" he argues that teachers should not only teach about empathy but provide students with opportunities to show what they come to believe about the value of helping others.

Teaching Kindness?

by Eric Walters

As I typed that two-word title, I paused, and then added a question mark. What was I possibly going to say in a few hundred words that would make that goal possible? Yet, the morning has just begun, the sun is still rising, and I am hopeful. So, let me try.

Empathy, simply put, involves the ability to understand the feelings of others. Muriel Rukeyser, American poet and activist, famously said, "The universe is made of stories, not atoms." I believe her. I believe stories are an integral part of who we are. We tell stories to entertain, educate, impact emotionally, and communicate. We have an inherent *need* to tell, and hear, stories.

In my picture books *My Name Is Blessing, Hope Springs*, and *Today Is the Day*, I tell stories inspired by the work I do in Kenya. They are about difficult truths and hopeful endings. These narratives are far removed from the day-to-day world of almost all of those who read the stories. I want them to see this other world, to understand other situations and other lives, and to spend a few moments inside another life. I often hear from teachers how these stories have emotionally affected their students — and them. Teachers will tell me that they were moved to tears. I often ask them what they are going to do with those tears. To quote from a famous song by Northern Lights in 1985 — "Tears Are Not Enough."

Empathy + Action = Kindness

As teachers, writers, and parents, we want to help our children understand the feelings and situations of others — especially those going through tragedy, trauma, and difficult life circumstances — but that's only the first step. If we take them only that far, we're not taking them far enough. We need to model for them acts of kindness, and further, allow them the opportunity to be kind. Once you read the book, what will you do about it? How do words and pictures become feelings and how do these feelings become actions?

I maintain that the most selfish thing you can do is help somebody — because it feels so good inside. And, when you do it once you're going to want to do it again, and again, and again. Allow students the opportunity to experience empathy and to act in kindness. Malala Yousafzai said, "One child, one teacher, one book, one pen can change the world."

You can be that teacher.

Books by Eric Walters That Promote Kindness and Resilience

Picture Books

Always with You; illus. Carloe Liu
From the Heart of Africa: A Book of Wisdom (ed.); illus. various
Light a Candle (with Godfrey Nkongolo); illus. Eva Campbell
The Matatu; illus. Eva Campbell
My Name Is Blessing; illus. Eugenie Fernandes
(Also: *Hope Springs*, *Today Is the Day*)
The Wild Beast; illus. Sue Todd

Novels

Bifocal (with Deborah Ellis)   *Shattered*
Broken Strings (with Kathy Kacer)   *Walking Home*
Elephant Secret   *We All Fall Down*
Shaken   *Wounded*

---

15 Events to Help Nurture a Caring Classroom Community

From *For a Better World: Reading and Writing for Social Action*

"Children need to be taught to and need to practice how to look at one another, how to talk to one another, not just perform for the teacher. They need to learn how to listen and respond to one another in a way that creates connections and builds a conversation history over time. They need to become interested in and accepting of differences and diversity in order to create a more democratic classroom environment."

— Randy Bomer and Katherine Bomer (2001, 46)

It's not so much what you do but how you do it that makes an event an opportunity to promote caring in the classroom. Consider how to take any of these suggestions and turn them into ways to help students grow in kindness and show caring.

Ideas to Explore

1. Implement interactive read-alouds *daily*.
2. Recognize opportunities to share personal stories (including yours as the teacher).
3. Create a class blog.
4. Celebrate learning with others in the community, for example, through drama presentations and curriculum projects.
5. Publish student writing to share within the school community and families.
6. Play cooperative games.
7. Identify and discuss hot topics drawn from news events.
8. Conduct class meetings to plan, develop, and reflect on learning events.

In *Creating Caring Classrooms*, Kathleen Gould Lundy and Larry Swartz outline 20 practices that represent important ways for teachers to establish a groundwork for creating a classroom as a community. (See pages 14 to 18.)

9. Celebrate birthdays.
10. Celebrate accomplishments, including random acts of kindness.
11. Plan and display an art show of student work.
12. Highlight a word-of-the-day each day.
13. Laugh — implement a joke of the day.
14. Organize a talent show.
15. Undertake a fundraising project.

Learning More About One Another

From *Other People's Children*

"In order to teach you, I must know you."

— Lisa Delpit (2006, 162)

At the beginning of the year, many teachers introduce getting-to-know-you activities with the goal of building a vibrant caring community. Autograph worksheets, cooperative games, and the telling of personal stories can help students learn more about the people they will be working alongside throughout the year. Such initiatives are not limited to the first weeks of September. Activities where students work, play, and share in pairs, in small groups, or as a whole class serve to help students make connections with and gain insights into others. In this way, the classroom becomes a microcosm for how students might socially engage with other people outside the classroom and in their adult lives.

Here are a few recommended activities designed to help students learn more about one another.

"That's Me!"

This game can be played with students sitting at their desks or arranged in a circle so they can notice one another. The teacher calls out different instructions and students shout out "That's me!" and stand if the instruction applies to them. As students stand, they are encouraged to notice others that they have something in common with. Alternatively, students, standing in a circle, can step forward if a statement applies to them.

Stand if . . .
> you were born in the summer.
> you have an older brother.
> you own a dog.
> you have won a prize.
> you have read more than one Harry Potter book.
> you can play a musical instrument.
> you have had stitches.
> you have recently travelled outside North America.

Extension

During a class meeting, students can share experiences and stories about one or more of the assigned "That's me!" topics to learn what they may or may not have in common with others.

"Tell Me Something About Yourself"

Ask the students to print their names in the centre of a piece of paper. In the top left-side corner, students list Accomplishments (I'm proud of . . .). In the top right-side corner, they identify My All-Time Favorite Book. In the bottom left-side corner, they list Possession(s) special to them. In the bottom right-side corner, they respond to "I Wish . . ."

ACCOMPLISHMENTS... (I'm proud of...) •My artistic abilities. • I never give up!	MY ALL TIME FAVOURITE BOOK... • Land of Stories series • Hunger Games series
POSSESSION... • My sketch book	I WISH... •to become a graphic Art/ designer • to have a good life

Once students have completed this, they hold the paper in front of them and walk around the room following teacher directions. To begin, they move without talking, reading as many profiles as they can in the allotted time. On a signal, students are told that they can talk with any people they meet about the listed items. The activity continues for several minutes so that students can interact with more than one player. Eventually, students form pairs and each student conducts an interview to learn more about their partner.

Working in groups of six or eight, students take turns to introduce their partners to the rest of the group.

Portrait Poems: Two Variations

For this activity, students create a list poem by completing several statements that will provide readers with a description of themselves or convey ideas about their interests, attitudes, beliefs, or feelings. Templates available on the Internet can inspire students to create poems that present self-portraits. The activity can be adapted to suit different grade levels by reducing the number of lines of the poem.

1. Students can choose from the list of sentence stems. Not all items need to be included in their poem.

An appealing alternative to this activity is to have students create "I am from . . ." list poems. Appalachian author George Ella Lyon's "I am . . ." poem could be used as a model. Students complete statements about favorite or special items (e.g., about foods, quotations, song lyrics, possessions, book titles, pastimes) repeating the sentence stem, "I am from . . ." to begin each line.

With thanks to Kathy Gould Lundy.

*I am . . .	I dream . . .	I worry . . .
I have . . .	I wonder . . .	I remember . . .
I like . . .	I try . . .	I approve . . .
I enjoy . . .	I believe . . .	I see . . .
I want . . .	I respect . . .	I hear . . .
I can . . .	I hope . . .	I feel . . .

*The first line could be repeated as the last line.
- Students can rearrange the order of the stems.
- They can write a list poem by repeating sentence stem items, providing a different descriptor for each statement.

I am Natasha.
I have brown eyes!
I have red hair.
I am kind.
I am helpful.
I love my fish.
I am caring.
I am Natasha.

- They can repeat some lines. For example, a poem can be divided into three or four stanzas with the final line of each stanza being the same.
- Once a first draft is completed, students can revise their writing by using vivid adverbs, adjectives, and synonyms to express an idea.
- Poems can be illustrated (or accompanied by a photograph) and displayed on a bulletin board, in a class blog, or in a cooperative class book where each student's writing is featured. A PowerPoint of portrait poems can be created with students each contributing one "I am" statement that describes them well.

2. A line master, "This Is Who I Am," is one template students can use to create portrait poems by finishing statements that describe them accurately. Students can replace any items with statements of their own choice. As students identify items that reveal who they are, they paint a picture in words about themselves.

The following poem is based on the template.

This Is Who I Am

I am a purring kitten, a roaring tiger.
I am the strum of a guitar, the blast of a trumpet.
I am the blue of faded blue jeans.

I enjoy finishing a great book.
I want to be known for being kind.
I pretend that I have the superpower of invisibility.
I believe that I should expect nothing and appreciate everything.
I dream about having a good life.
I wonder about tomorrow.

I am the falling, swirling leaves of Autumn.
I am sometimes a whisper, sometimes a shout.
I am confident, ambitious, thoughtful.

My name is Zoe.

A Story Behind Every Name

From *My Name Is Blessing* by Eric Walters

"You want me to change my name?" Muthini asked.

"I want *you* to change your *future*," Gabriel replied. "I can never look at you and see suffering and I don't want other to see it either. I want them to hear your name and see what I see, what your Nyanya sees: a blessing. Baraka."

In her research, Belarie Zatzman reminds us that "our names are artifacts of our identities." Everyone has a name. Behind every name is a story. To begin, students can turn to one or two classmates to tell a story about their name. The following questions, displayed on a chart, can be used to guide the discussion:

What is the meaning behind your name?
Why did your parents choose to give you this name?
Were you named after someone?
Do you have more than one name?
Do you have a nickname?
Do you like your name?
Do you know your name in other languages?
If you could choose another name, what might it be? Why?
What, if anything, is unique about the spelling of your first name? of your last name?

As students listen to the sharing of other name stories, they come to recognize the diversity of their identities and this sharing can contribute to the building of community.

This Is Who I Am

My name is _____

I am . . . (the animal that best represents me)

I am . . . (the musical instrument that best represents me)

I am . . . (a color that best represents me)

I enjoy . . . (a favorite pastime, hobby, or sport)

I want . . . (something I'd like to own, something I'd like to have)

I pretend . . . (something I'd like to be or do)

I believe . . . (a favorite saying, expression, or song lyric)

I dream about . . . (a wish or a hope for the present or my future life)

I wonder about . . . (a topic or theme to do with the world)

I am . . . (the season that best represents me)

I am . . . (the sound that best represents me)

I am . . . (two or three adjectives that best describe me)

My name is _____

Pembroke Publishers © 2020 *Teaching Tough Topics* by Larry Swartz   ISBN 978-1-55138-341-5

- To build a sense of classroom community, give each student an opportunity to tell a part of their name story. Sitting in a circle, each student shares a narrative connected to their name.
- Invite some students to find more information about their names by using the Internet or asking questions of family members.
- Ask students to write their name stories to share with others. The stories could be published on a class website.
- Suggest that students investigate and present the name stories of other family members.

Grade 6 student examples:

"My name is Mia and I love it. My parents were going to name me Summer because I was born on summer solstice. I'm glad they named me Mia."

"Once upon a time there was a kid blessed by God, and thus was born Adam."

"My name is Georgia. In Latin it means 'farmer's daughter.' My parents chose the name because my dad LOVES music (Me too!). When my mom was thinking of girl names, she thought of Georgia and of course my dad loved it because of the jazzy song, 'Georgia on My Mind.'"

Some Picture Books About Names

Alexie, Sherman (illus. Yuyi Morales). *Thunder Boy Jr.*
Choi, Yangsook. *The Name Jar*
Henkes, Kevin. *Chrysanthemum*
Martinez-Neal, Juana. *Alma and How She Got Her Name*
Mobin-Uddin, Asma (illus. Barbara Kiwak). *My Name Is Bilal*
Recorvits, Helen (illus. Gabi Swiatkowska). *My Name Is Yoon*

Alma and How She Got Her Name is a 2018 picture book that won the Caldecott Medal.

Practising Kindness

From *Just Because It's Not Wrong Doesn't Make It Right*

"If we are to raise kids who think and act ethically, we don't begin with the thinking or the acting. We begin with the caring."

— Barbara Coloroso (2012)

Words Worth Quoting

The activities outlined below provide strategies for students to respond to quotations about kindness, given on page 154. Teachers may choose among them.

1. *Respond to a quotation.*

    Students choose one of the quotations and write a short response guided by one or more of the following questions:

    Why did you choose this quotation?

    What does this quotation invite you to think about?

    What does this quotation mean?

    How is this statement significant to the theme of practising kindness?

2. *Make an inquiry about the quotation.*
   Students can gather research. What can they discover about the person who said or wrote this statement? They may find information about why the quotation was created, when it was said, and who the audience was.
3. *Prioritize quotations by significance.*
   Students independently choose one or two favorite quotations about practising kindness from the list. Then, working in groups of five or six, with each student contributing a different quotation, students prioritize the items by listing the most significant to the least significant. Groups can then share their choices with others.

   The whole class discusses and determines which quotation best sums up the purpose and goals of the classroom community. In a sense, the class is setting a mission statement.
4. *Put a quotation on display.*
   Each student chooses a quotation and creates a banner or poster to visually display it in the classroom or the school.
5. *Research quotations that matter to others.*
   Many people have a personal statement that serves as a philosophy of life. For example, my current mantra is "Expect nothing — appreciate everything." The statement might be something a parent or grandparent has repeated, or it might be a quotation that they have read or heard about from the media. For a research project, students can interview one or two adults in the school community or in their family to discover their favorite and why it is important to them. Have students report their findings in a class meeting.

Spreading Kindness

Share the following small news story about a random act of kindness:

On August 27, 2019, a young boy, like many youngsters, was overwhelmed with the first day of school. Another boy, eight-year-old Christian Moore, was also heading into the school in Wichita, Kansas, when he noticed the distressed boy curled up in a ball crying as he sat outside the corner of his school. Christian went over to the boy and comforted him. He then took the hand of the troubled boy and walked him safely into the school. Christian was unaware that the distressed eight-year-old boy, Connor Crites, had autism.

What are some ways that we can show kindness?

Suggestion #1: Provide students with a large sheet of paper. Have students, working in groups, make a list of different ways that we can be kind to others. Encourage students to think of ways that they have been kind to others and others have been kind to them.

As a class, compile and display a list of ways to be kind to others.

Suggestion #2: Provide students with a copy of the "Spreading Kindness" line master on page 155. This list suggests ways to help students think about how they have been kind to others and to raise awareness and set goals of showing new ways to be kind to others.

Extension: Choose at least one way of offering kindness from the "Spreading Kindness" line master. Make that a goal for a week, encouraging students to implement a random act of kindness to someone.

"If one person is unhappy, we are all unhappy."

— Toshiro Kanamori, Japanese teacher, from *Children Full of Life*, a documentary film

In the novel *Wonder* by R. J. Palacio, Auggie Pullman's classroom teacher, Mr. Browne, inspires his students by presenting precepts to engage and enlighten them. Beyond that, the book *365 Days of Wonder* (edited by R. J. Palacio) features a memorable quotation about courage, friendship, love, or kindness for every day of the year.

"The best way to find yourself is to lose yourself in the service of others."

— Mahatma Gandhi

The picture book *A World of Kindness* from the editors and illustrators of Pajama Press presents evocative questions about how children might show kindness and consideration for others. For example: "Could you share something special?" "When someone is shy, do you help her join in?"

Be Kind to One Another: Quotations for Reflection

"Kind words can be short and easy to speak, but their echoes are truly endless."
— Mother Teresa

"Be the change that you wish to see in the world."
— Mahatma Gandhi

"Never doubt that a small group of thoughtful, committed citizens can change the world; indeed, it's the only thing that ever has."
— Margaret Mead

"If you have a choice between being right and being kind, choose kind."
— Dr. Wayne W. Dwyer

"You cannot do a kindness too soon, for you never know how soon it will be too late."
— Ralph Waldo Emerson

"Well done is better than well said."
—Benjamin Franklin

"Carry out a random act of kindness, with no expectation of reward, safe in the knowledge that one day someone might do the same for you."
— Lady Diana Spencer

"We must not seek to defeat or humiliate an opponent but to win friendship and understanding . . . every word and deed must contribute to an understanding."
— Dr. Martin Luther King Jr.

"How wonderful it is that nobody need wait a single moment before starting to improve the world."
— Anne Frank

My friends, love is better than anger. Hope is better than fear. Optimism is better than despair. So let us be loving, hopeful and optimistic. And we'll change the world.
— Jack Layton

"Once you witness an injustice, you are no longer an observer but a participant."
— June Callwood

"When I was a boy and I would see scary things in the news, my mother would say to me, 'Look for the helpers. You will always find people who are helping.'"
— Fred Rogers

"Do things for people not because of who they are or what they do in return, but because of who you are."
— Harold S. Kushner

"A single act of kindness throws out roots in all directions, and the roots spring up and make new trees."
— Amelia Earhart

"You can see yourself as the wave in the ocean or you can see yourself as the ocean."
— Oprah Winfrey

"We do not really see through our eyes or hear through our ears, but through our beliefs."
— Lisa Delpit

"Kindness is difficult to give away because it keeps coming back."
— Marcel Proust

Pembroke Publishers © 2020 *Teaching Tough Topics* by Larry Swartz   ISBN 978-1-55138-341-5

Spreading Kindness

Part A

The following statements represent ways to be kind to others. Review the list. How have you shown kindness recently? Check five items. Now put a star beside two or three items to act on in the next two weeks.

_____ Listen.

_____ Pay a compliment.

_____ Offer to help someone.

_____ Say "please" and "thank you."

_____ Send an email or paper note of thanks.

_____ Invite someone to be part of your group.

_____ Say "Hello!" or "Good morning!"

_____ Smile.

_____ Tell a story.

_____ Ask someone to tell you a story.

_____ Share equipment, perhaps a pencil, an eraser, or an unused Kleenex.

_____ Share a snack.

_____ Hold a door open for someone.

_____ Lend a book.

_____ Lend a hand.

_____ Notice (and praise) an article of clothing someone is wearing.

_____ Don't be a bystander!

_____ Make a donation.

_____ Applaud the effort someone has taken.

_____ Spread kindness like confetti . . .

Other _____

Part B

One kind thing I have recently done is _____

Something kind that someone has done to me (or someone else) was

_____

One thing I might do to show kindness is_____

"I Am Doing Everything I Can!"

When situations are daunting — tough — it is worthwhile, even essential, to live a life according to kindness and positivity. There are those who see the glass as half full and those who see it as half empty. There are those who remain passive and those who, after consideration, take action. People concerned about achieving social justice and equity are those who will show kindness and positivity by taking action.

A story about a hummingbird can serve to help confirm or challenge student assumptions about what to do when hard decisions confront them. The story of the hummingbird striving to put out a forest fire has been told by the Quechua people of Ecuador and Peru. While other animals stand by, bemoaning their inability to stop the fire, the hummingbird fearlessly fights it. Never discouraged, Hummingbird demonstrates that it is not always the largest or the loudest that can do the most good. Her efforts remind us that the one who is not afraid to act can make the biggest difference. At the least, she reminds us that striving to do something good is worthwhile.

A Canadian picture book version of the hummingbird story has been created by Michael Nicoll Yahgulanaas, a Haida artist. The Tsimshian people of the North Pacific recognize the hummingbird to be a joyful messenger, delivering hope and healing during times of sorrow and pain. (See the Haida anime "Flight of the Hummingbird" by Michael Nicoll Yahgulanaas on YouTube.)

At an annual Botanic Gardens Conservation International conference, Noble Peace Prize laureate Wangari Maathai shared a version of this inspirational story when she addressed 7000 educators from around the world in Montreal. Although this story can be seen as a parable for the environment, as noted in the picture book version, it applies well to the effort of addressing any tough topics such as are explored in this resource.

A Readers theatre version of "The Little Hummingbird" appears on page 158. In Readers theatre, students are assigned parts and rehearse a script to present it well to an audience. For this activity, it is suggested that several medium-sized groups form. In each group, three narrators can be used to help tell the story; however, the narrator role could be distributed among four or five students. Once students have their parts, they rehearse an effective way to present the tale. Sound effects and gestures can be added, but with Readers theatre, participants are not required to memorize or act out the text.

Responding to "The Little Hummingbird"

• Discussing

The following key questions can be used to guide a discussion about the story.
  What lesson do you think can be learned from this story?
  Do you think Hummingbird's efforts to put out the fire were foolish? Why?
  What puzzles or questions come to mind?
  What does the statement "I am doing everything I can!" mean to you?
  In what real-life ways can we put Hummingbird's philosophy into action?

• Illustrating

Students can create an illustration that they think could be used for a picture book version of this story. Student images can be assembled into a class presentation for others to read. One suggestion is to do torn-paper art, where students use a variety of colored papers to create a scene — no scissors allowed.

- *Dramatizing*

Students can work in groups of four or five to dramatize the story. Tableaux, movement, narration, and improvisation can be explored to tell the story of the tiny hummingbird dramatically.

"The Little Hummingbird" serves as a vehicle for students to think about taking action, offering help, and being kind to one another. The story is intended to leave the students thinking, "What would I do?" Here are some thoughts by Grade 5 students:

> "The hummingbird was great and thoughtful for trying to make a difference even though he might do anything helpful, he at least attempted to do so."

> "Some people might think the hummingbird is crazy. Some people might think he was brave. I'm going to take the hummingbird's point of view. If my home caught on fire, and I lost everything I loved, I would want to help, and do all I could. If you were the bird, would you feel the same?"

> "If you don't think that you can do anything, then you will live a miserable life. You need to always, always do what you can."

Will Students Be Inspired to Act?

In *Reading to Make a Difference*, Lester L. Laminack and Katie Kelly present an essential need for students to react individually or collectively in ways that can make a difference. Working inside and outside a tough topic, as well as encountering literature that helps readers think about issues and deepens their understanding of social justice, equity, and diversity, is a good place to start. But, after experiencing a piece of literature, how might students be changed? In what ways might students be inspired to act, to make a positive difference, to spread ripples of kindness drop by drop by drop?

Ask: "Are you a bear, a snake, an owl — or a hummingbird?"

From *Reading to Make a Difference*

"If we are changed by what we read and the experiences that broaden our world view one action does bring this to closure. We want to cultivate students as thoughtful caring citizens and lifelong agents of change. We believe this work should be ongoing and organically embedded into the classroom routines, instruction, classroom culture, and lives of students."

— Lester L. Laminack and Katie Kelly (2019, xx)

The Little Hummingbird: Readers Theatre

SNAKE: The forest is on fire!

OWL: The forest is on fire!

BEAR: The forest is on fire!

NARRATOR 1: A terrible fire had been burning and burning for two days and two nights.

NARRATOR 2: All the birds and all the animals raced to escape the raging flames and clouds of dark smoke.

SNAKE: The fire's so wild! What can I do except slither?

OWL: The fire is everywhere! Where should I fly?

BEAR: The fire can harm us! My fur will get frazzled and frizzy.

NARRATOR 1: The animals huddled by the edge of a nearby stream and looked back in silence. They sadly watched the blazing fire destroy their homes.

Together the animals heave a deep sigh.

NARRATOR 2: How sad and frightened and powerless each of the creatures felt.

NARRATOR 3: Except for one brave hummingbird . . .

NARRATOR 1: The tiny bird decided she had to do something to help.

NARRATOR 2: She swooped into the stream and picked a single drop of water with her needle-like beak.

NARRATOR 3: She swiftly returned to the forest and dropped the drop onto the fire.

NARRATOR 1: She flew back to the stream and gathered another drop of water.

NARRATORS 1, 2, 3: Back and forth, back and forth, back and forth she flew.

NARRATOR 1: The forest animals watched in disbelief as the courageous hummingbird continued her mission.

NARRATOR 2: . . . drop by drop by drop.

SNAKE: Why are you wasting your time?

OWL: Why are you flying where your wings will burn?

BEAR: Why are you fighting a fire that won't stop?

NARRATOR 1: The animals stood around and stared as Hummingbird kept gathering drops of water . . .

NARRATOR 2: . . . one by one by one.

NARRATOR 3: How hopeless they looked and how baffled they all felt by Hummingbird's actions!

OWL: Hummingbird, what do you think you're doing? The fire is so big, and you are so little.

NARRATOR 1: Hummingbird did not stop to answer.

NARRATOR 2: Without losing a beat of her wings, she looked back and said

HUMMINGBIRD: *I am doing everything I can!*

NARRATORS AND CREATURES: She is doing everything she can!

Pembroke Publishers © 2020 *Teaching Tough Topics* by Larry Swartz ISBN 978-1-55138-341-5

Great Books About Kindness, Caring, and Connecting

Picture Books

From *Willa's House* by David Booth

Isn't it strange how, on a summer's night,
Willa could sit alone on the porch on this busy street,
filled with car horns and squealing tires, and still feel
the smallness of the town, the peace of the neighbourhood, the
safety of her home, the hope of the world,
all wrapped in the memories that filled Willa's house.

Atkinson, Cale. *Where Oliver Fits*

Berger, Carin. *All of Us*

Booth, David (illus. Renia Metallinou). *Willa's House*

Britt, Paige (illus. Sean Qualls and Selina Alko). *Why Am I Me?*

Deedy, Carmen Agra, with Wilson Kimeli Naiyomah (illus. Thomas Gonzales). *14 Cows for America*

Fitch, Sheree (illus. Emma Fitzgerald). *Everybody's Different on Everybody Street*

Fox, Mem (illus. Leslie Staub). *Whoever You Are*

Jeffers, Oliver. *Here We Are: Notes for Living on Planet Earth*

Jenkins, Kathryn. *Inclusion Alphabet: ABC's for Everyone*

Kang, Anna (illus. Christopher Weyant). *We Are (Not) Friends*

Kostecki-Shaw, Jenny Sue. *Same, Same But Different*

Lawson, JonArno (illus. Sydney Smith). *Sidewalk Flowers*

Leannah, Michael (illus. Jennifer E. Morris). *Most People*

Mackesy, Charles. *The Boy, the Mole, the Fox, and the Horse*

Miller, Pat Zietlow (illus. Jen Hill). *Be Kind*

Pajama Press, eds. *A World of Kindness*

Penfold, Alexandra (illus. Suzanne Kaufman). *All Are Welcome*

Pollak, Barbara. *Our Community Garden*

Reynolds, Peter H. *Say Something!*

Siers, Sophie (illus. Anne Villeneuve). *Dear Mr. President*

Smith, Monique Gray (illus. Danielle Daniel). *You Hold Me Up*

Yousafzai, Malala (illus. Kerascoët). *Malala's Magic Pencil*

Woodson, Jacqueline (illus. E. B. Lewis). *Each Kindness*

Bibliography

Bomer, Randy, and Katherine Bomer. 2001. *For a Better World: Reading and Writing for Social Action.* Portsmouth, NH: Heinemann.

Booth, David. 1992. *Censorship Goes to School.* Markham, ON: Pembroke.

_____. 2016. *Literacy 101.* Markham, ON: Pembroke.

Botelho, Maria José, and Masha Kabakow Rudman. 2009. *Critical Multicultural Analysis of Children's Literature: Mirrors, Windows, and Doors.* New York: Routledge.

Coloroso, Barbara. 2003. *The Bully, the Bullied, and the Bystander.* New York: HarperCollins.

_____. 2012. *Just Because It's Not Wrong Doesn't Make It Right: Teaching Kids to Think and Act Ethically.* Toronto: Penguin Canada.

Delpit, Lisa. 2006. *Other People's Children: Cultural Conflict in the Classroom.* New York: The New Press.

_____. 2013. *"Multiplication Is for White People": Raising Expectations for Other People's Children.* New York: The New Press.

Ellis, Deborah. 2019. "Creating a Day Before." [IBBY] *Bookbird* 57 (1): 1–13.

Fitch, Sheree, and Larry Swartz. 2008. *The Poetry Experience.* Markham, ON: Pembroke.

Hope, Julia. 2008. "'One Day We Had to Run': The Development of the Refugee Identity in Children's Literature and Its Function in Education." *Children's Literature in Education* 39 (4): 295–304.

Laminack, Lester L., and Katie Kelley. 2019. *Reading to Make a Difference: Using Literature to Help Students Speak Freely, Think Deeply and Take Action.* Portsmouth, NH: Heinemann.

Landt, Susan M. 2006. "Multicultural Literature and Young Adolescents: A Kaleidoscope of Opportunity." *Journal of Adolescent & Adult Literacy* 49 (8): 690–97.

Lundy, Kathleen Gould. 2015. *Conquering the Crowded Curriculum.* Markham, ON: Pembroke.

_____. 2019. *Stand Up and Teach.* Markham, ON: Pembroke.

_____. 2020. *Teaching Fairly in an Unfair World*, 2nd ed. Markham, ON: Pembroke.

Lundy, Kathleen Gould, and Larry Swartz. 2011. *Creating Caring Classrooms.* Markham, ON: Pembroke.

Meek, Margaret, ed. 2001. *Children's Literature and National Identity.* Staffordshire, UK: Trentham Books.

Miller, Donalyn. 2009. *The Book Whisperer: Awakening the Inner Reader in Every Child.* San Francisco: Jossey-Bass.

Paul, Pamela, and Maria Russo. 2019. *How to Raise a Reader.* New York: Workman.

Pepler, Debra, and Wendy Craig. 2000. *Making a Difference in Bullying.* The Melissa Institute: http://www.melissainstitute.org/documents/ MakingADifference.pdf.

Roberts, Ceri. 2017. *Refugees and Migrants.* Illustrated by Hanane Kai. Hauppauge, NY: Barron Educational Series.

Rowsell, Jennifer. 2017. "Passing Through: Reflecting on the Journey Through Community Arts Zone." *Pedagogies: An International Journal* 12 (1): 1–3.

Souto-Manning, Marianna, and Jessica Martell. 2016. *Reading, Writing, and Talk: Inclusive Teaching Strategies for Diverse Learners, K–2.* New York: Teachers College Press.

Swartz, Larry. 2015. *Dramathemes*, 4th ed. Markham, ON: Pembroke.

_____. 2017. *Take Me to Your Readers.* Markham, ON: Pembroke.

Swartz, Larry, and Shelley Stagg Peterson. 2015. *"This Is a Great Book!"* Markham, ON: Pembroke.

Wilhelm, Jeffrey D., Peggy Jo Wilhelm, and Erika Boas. 2009. *Inquiring Minds: Learn to Read and Write: 50 Problem-Based Literacy & Learning Strategies.* Oakville, ON: Rubicon.

Index

8325

recognizing and respecting children, 95
storytelling, 99–101
student perceptions, 99
word choice, 96–97

questions/questioning
brainstorming, 88, 90
discussion and quiz, 75–76
generating, 78
identity, 116
novel as impetus, 86–90
range of questions, 74–78
reading comprehension, 88
report planning and delivery, 76, 78
quotations, 152–53

race/racism
anti-discriminatory teaching, 26
books, 36, 38–39
challenging, 26–27
children and, 26
definitions, 29, 30
early conversations about, 27
monologue, 34–36
picture book, 31–34
scenarios, 30
talking about, 25
racial literacy, 26–27
racist, 29
Readers theatre, 156, 158
reading comprehension, 88
refugee experience
books, 50–51
definitions, 43
discussing, 44–45
global refugee crisis, 41–42
graphic organizers, 44–45
graphic page, 48–50
language and vocabulary, 43
picture book, 44–48
teaching about, 42–43
written response, 44
relational bullying, 134
religion, 12, 14, 24, 67, 75–76, 106, 113, 122
remembrance
bereavement, 107–8
books, 106, 113–14
definitions, 108
diversity, 109

encounters with death, 106–7
family experiences, 113
honoring death, 112–13
language and vocabulary, 108–9
making connections, 109
oral narratives, 109, 111–12
protecting children, 105–7
research, 113
reports, 76, 78
residential schools, 55
Responding to a Picture Book, 126
Responding to a Poem, 144
response activities
benefits, 19
described, 19–20
Indigenous identities, 63–64
tough topics, 20
retelling, 100

semantic mapping, 83–84
sex, 118–19
sexual orientation, 119
singing/songs, 64
Sixties Scoop, 54
Skin, 37
snippets, 142
social class, 93
social justice, 81, 93
Spreading Kindness, 155
story mapping, 64
storytelling, 99–101

T-chart, 45
tableaux
described, 46
exploring picture books through, 45–48
extensions, 47–48
graphic pages and, 50
working inside and outside, 46–47
Teachings of the Seven Grandfathers, 63
"Tell Me Something About Yourself," 148–49
text-message conversations, 139
text-to-text connections, 60
"That's Me!", 148
"The class photo that made a father cry," 87
The Little Hummingbird: Readers Theatre, 158

think-alouds, 61–63
Thinking About Homophobia, 122–23
Thinking About My Fiction Choices, 33
Thinking About Racism: What If . . .?, 32
thinking stems, 31–34
"This History Must Be Taught," 58
This Is Who I Am, 151
title, 9
tough topics
books, 12–13, 36, 38–39, 50–51, 64–66, 78–79, 90–91
bullying, 11
death, 10–11
described, 10
gender stereotypes, 11
helping students make sense of, 11–12
Holocaust, 67–79
immigrant and refugee experience, 40–51
Indigenous identities, 52–66
multicultural literature and, 13–14
multimodal expression, 20
physical and mental challenges, 80–91
race and diversity, 23–39
reasons for teaching, 10
strategies, 21
when to teach, 10–12
Turtle Island, 54

upstanders, 134

visualizing, 60
Voices in the Head, 47

writing in role, 103, 129

young adult books
death, loss, and remembrance, 114
gender identity and homophobia, 130
Holocaust, 79
Indigenous identities, 66
poverty, 104
race/diversity, 39